NURSE!

Thirty-Eight Years a Nurse

Being the Best I Can Be!

Louise Giles

FIRST EDITION

ISBN
eBook: 978-1-80227-447-9
Paperback: 978-1-80227-446-2

"We need women who are so strong they can be gentle, so educated they can be humble, so fierce they can be compassionate, so passionate they can be rational and so disciplined they can be free."

Kavita Ramdas

Contents

In line with the Nursing & Midwifery Code (NMC, 2018), every attempt has been made to maintain confidentiality by excluding names of places and people though some may recognise themselves.

Louise Giles, RGN, MA(Ed), PGDip, BSc (Hons), FNF Scholar, SFHEA.

Foreword

As Director of the Royal College of Nursing Wales, I am delighted to introduce this wonderful memoir. Louise's personal and insightful perspective on her nursing career is published during an unprecedented time in the United Kingdom and, indeed, globally. COVID-19 hit us like a freight train and is unlike anything we have experienced in modern times. Like many nurses across the country, Louise acknowledges the challenge of the pandemic and how it has changed all our lives.

Nursing is a dynamic profession, making a significant contribution to health care which is constantly evolving. It is critical that registered nurses keep apprised of research, technology and new ways of working to deliver excellent patient care. However, this is a constant challenge, and nurses must often fight for investment into their continuing professional development and mandatory training that is essential to carry out their roles. Furthermore, nurses are underpaid and therefore, nursing teams are understaffed in our National Health Service, which Louise describes as the 'most amazing organisation in the world.' The stress and demands can be overwhelming, with many telling tell me they don't have enough time to spend with patients.

Nursing is a vital part of the care we all receive throughout our lifespan. Louise explores her varied roles as a clinician and an educator and details her continuous learning journey. She explains it beautifully when she writes that she wants her readers to understand how it feels to be a nurse, the importance of knowledge and of making the best use of every single life experience.

Nurses have a long history of extraordinary leadership in very difficult times, including war, pandemics and natural disasters. Nursing is a tremendously rewarding profession. I qualified as a nurse in 1996, and it remains one of the best decisions I've ever made, alongside working with and learning from Louise. It is an honour and a privilege to be trusted with the care of patients and clients. This memoir captures the challenges and incredible rewards of the role and will become an essential record of the voice of nursing.

Helen Whyley

Introduction

The COVID pandemic offered many challenges to people everywhere, and my world has certainly changed in light of the virus. However, every cloud has a silver lining and my pre-lockdown rendezvous with an author led to me writing this book and, in doing so, thinking long and hard about my life, career, family and friends.

This book is not intended to teach you how to be a nurse but may help in your understanding of how it feels to be one and how important it is to learn and make the best use of every single experience in our life.

At the age of eighteen, my career as a nurse commenced on a dreary Sunday afternoon, arriving in the nurses' home with boxes and bags. My accommodation block was a long, single-storey, brick-built building with a corrugated roof and single-glazed windows. There were 15 single rooms on either side of a long corridor and two bathrooms and toilets at the end, opposite a kitchen and sitting room.

I know my mother did not want to leave me there, though she didn't tell me so at the time.

I could not help and wonder what this was going to be like. The nurses' home was within easy walking distance of the School of Nursing and the hospital, and so our March 1984 cohort of student nurses quickly became a part of the NHS community.

The questions and concerns of the student nurses that I work with, some thirty-eight years later, remain the same as those that I had back in 1984. You just want to know everything, experience everything and get out there to be a nurse. For an eighteen-year-old, it was an exciting adventure.

Writing this book is to share my experiences, reflect upon learning and enable you, the reader, to consider how you can be the very best you can be.

Whilst we live in a world of exposure to social media and all that is available via the web, there remains something truly magical about simply sharing stories. Within Wales (where most of my nursing career has been spent thus far), we have a rich tradition of poetry and prose, dating back to the sixth century. Oral storytelling has thrived, so folk tales have been passed from generation to generation. Telling stories in person can enable improvisation and a change in response to the audience – many people do this through acting, singing and storytelling. In my teaching, and through the facilitation of structured reflection, I am able to both listen to stories and tell mine – this can bring to life the subject matter we are dealing with. Of course, during the pandemic of COVID-19, we have had to adapt our teaching, delivering so much more than ever before online. This has meant that storytelling and facilitation needed to be adapted for synchronous and asynchronous teaching.

I believe storytelling is a part of all of us and can help strengthen our communities. By sharing my stories, I hope that I can support learning and education in the nursing community.

Chapter One

Starting Out

"While there may be a place for intuition in the art of nursing, there is no place in the science of nursing for ritual and mythology."

—Walsh & Ford

At the tender age of eighteen, did I even know what nursing was all about? I had only ever visited family in hospital on a couple of occasions and was pretty sure that I didn't see anything that I remember, but somehow, I just knew that nursing was for me. I guess this was the desire to help and care for others, and that aspiration remains with me.

What did I bring from my young life that might enable me to cope with being a student nurse in 1984? I had no experience of hospital or care work, but I knew what it was to care for others and how important kindness is to everyone - especially so when we are vulnerable.

My upbringing was very straightforward up to the age of eleven: mother, father, 2.5 children and a dog (well, three children and a cat!). However, things were to change when, all in the space of a British summer, I left primary school, my mother left the family home, and I started secondary school.

My father was an ordinary man from the north of England who smoked heavily, having done so since he was a teenager, and he drank beer most weekends. These were two habits that he never gave up. He was one of ten, seven brothers and two sisters, and he worked hard all his life. I never knew him not to go to work right up until his admission to hospital with cancer of the oesophagus, his two habits being the death of him.

My mother was a normal mum. She is short in height but big in attitude, although when I was young, I thought she was very quiet; actually, she is still quiet but gets her point across in other ways. She was the eldest of four girls and lost her father when she was thirteen, she then looked after her sisters whilst my grandmother went out to work. She was only seventeen when she married my dad, and whilst that was very common back then, I cannot help but wonder if she was truly happy. She fell in love with a friend of my father, and after a couple of stalled attempts to leave, she did break free to make a new life for herself.

In 1977, 'broken families' were a rare thing; indeed, I did not know anyone else who this had happened to. My secondary school years were difficult for me without my mother at home. My brother was leaving home, my sister was doing her own thing, and I was not really happy with my father's choices regarding his relationships and eventually losing the family home. It became clear to me that my mother had been the glue that held the family together, and once she had gone, things started to fall apart. Nonetheless, with the support of family and friends, we all survived. I developed a determination in my early teenage years to make my own way in life and do everything I wanted when I wanted to do it.

At the age of fourteen, I decided nursing was for me, so I chose the options I needed for my O-levels. Maths, English and a science were required for nursing: a minimum of five O-levels in total. I chose biology, chemistry, history, home economics (I love cooking and eating), English literature (I love reading) and typewriting (because the other options were French or geography) and achieved the grades required at sixteen. These two years really were about me growing into an independent young woman with very little guidance from my parents. Hence I chose subjects that I liked, but who knew how useful being able to touch-type would be throughout my working life and future learning? During these years, I also cemented a lifelong friendship with my one friend at that time. We have gone on to enjoy high days and holidays together and be godmothers to one another's children.

Back then, there were no A levels required for a pre-registration nursing course, so I was off to earn a living! I followed the daughter of a family friend, who was a mother's help, to the bright lights of London, where I worked for two years with a family, caring for their four children.

The family lived in Finchley, and Mr B was 'something in the city.' I did not really understand what that meant at the time, but I guess it was banking. Mrs B was always busy and very sociable, plus a phenomenal cook; I learnt so much from her. Two of the children lived at home, and the other two came to us most weekends and during the holidays. I grew to love them all and keep in touch, following them on social media to know what they are up to, and I enjoy sharing their grown-up lives.

The London experience taught me so many things, not least that 'broken families' can happen no matter where you live or your background, and that this experience need not shape you in a negative sense. My time in London showed me that my kind and caring nature was important in the engagement of others. These two years exposed me to wealth that I did not know existed, food I had never eaten and opportunities to travel that built my confidence and ensured my determination to work hard and build a future. I would grow from my working-class roots and ensure I built a happy, warm and comfortable home with full food cupboards and a holiday savings pot.

Returning to Wales, leaving my second family behind, was hard, but I was so excited to take the next steps. The children cried, I cried, and Mrs B said, "Loulou, if I have another baby, will you stay?!"

1984 was quite a year – not all that Orwell predicted, thankfully, however a lot of things were happening. Branson launched Virgin Atlantic; Prince owned the summer with Purple Rain, the film and the album; HIV was identified as the cause of AIDS; the Mineworkers Union took the miners on strike for a year whilst Thatcher ruled with an iron fist: Madonna performed her *'Like a Virgin'* song live for the first time, and Band Aid released *'Do They Know It's Christmas?'*

Life as a student nurse was very different in 1984 than it is for the students that I work with now. We were employed by the hospital and paid a wage each month, and we were rostered to work alongside the rest of the nursing team on the wards, in departments and in community settings. Of course, many changes had occurred already, as many of my friends who started just a few short years before told me.

Not long before 1984, there were many Draconian measures in place. You could not be a student nurse if you were married; if you became pregnant, you had to leave the course; you had to be in the nurse's home in time for the curfew and doors locked. Some of my friends would regularly escape and re-enter via a bedroom window - I imagine it was like a scene from a Carry On film!

We had our first six weeks in school learning all the fundamentals of care and practising skills on one another. Why would I volunteer to let my colleagues practice passing a nasogastric tube on me? Why didn't I put my hand up for having my teeth brushed? That seemed a little less invasive! We pushed one another around the grounds in wheelchairs, guided each other along blindfolded, fed each other lunch in the canteen and studied Ross & Wilson's *Anatomy and Physiology* book until we could almost recite it word for word.

So it was that we ventured to our first wards: ten weeks of a variety of shifts dressed in our white dresses, white tights and white shoes with our hair tied up and a white cardboard hat popped on top - one yellow stripe for a first-year student. It was nothing like the sexy image some may have of nurses' uniforms, and certainly not as shown in *Carry On Nurse*.

A nerve-wracking time was when Sister took you into the office to tell you how things worked and what was expected of you. I can remember her as if it was yesterday - Sister Jones; she was tiny in stature but nonetheless a little scary as she checked my uniform, fingernails, and handwashing technique. She led by example, though, as she was always professional and proper in her uniform and behaviour.

I often wondered if the Sisters I met in those early years ever used their Christian names. I certainly never heard them addressed other than 'Sister' by everyone, so I never knew any of their names.

Handover on the ward took place in the office, no-one wrote anything down; we listened intently to the information about each patient and waited to be allocated our roles for the shift. No-one sat down in the office until Sister sat down, and if Matron should call to the ward, we all stood up immediately. Respect or fear? I never felt anything other than respect for these experienced nurses. They were serious, sometimes stern, but they always had the answer and were available to direct and support. Here I was, learning from role models before I knew what leadership and role modelling were.

On my very first day on this female medical ward, I saw my first dead person. I was not with the patient when she died; that role was undertaken by the third-year student on the ward. She was only a couple of years older than me, but she seemed so confident, and I was totally in awe of her.

How did she know what to do? When the family had left, I went with the third-year student and the staff nurse to perform last offices. I was more than a little scared; I had seen what to do in my six weeks in school, but this was a real person. I was touched by the vase of flowers, the bible and the tea tray that had been provided for the family. The eighty-year-old lady looked peaceful, and I was unprepared for the caring and dignified way in which the nurses spoke to her as they washed her. Whilst packing of the orifices (not a practice that happens anymore) was a little undignified, it was done so carefully and with kindness that I had a sense that she would not have minded.

"There you go, Mrs Jones, all packed up and ready to go to Rose Cottage (a term used when referring to the mortuary) - rest easy."

This approach and the opening of a window to allow the release of the soul have been practices that seemed, on one hand, parochial and non-sensical, but on the other hand, caring, kind and quite beautiful.

The practice of last offices is not the only practice to have changed dramatically over the years. Some of the rituals incorporated in the nurse's role have long since been eradicated as a result of research and evidence-based practice. In the last 20-30 years, the length of hospital stay has decreased dramatically for most people. Indeed, many hospital admissions that resulted in a stay of a week or more would not even be considered for admissions now. So, mothers would stay in bed for 5-10 days postnatally before being 'allowed' up and now some will be home within 5-10 hours! People would be admitted for cataracts, carpal tunnel, varicose vein surgery, yet today, these procedures are undertaken as day surgery. People with back pain might have been admitted for bed rest and traction; now, they will attend a walk-in clinic at a physiotherapy outpatient department as a self-referral.

Changes in services and expectations of the public, as well as modernisation and research, drive many changes.

Some nursing practices have altered as we have become increasingly aware of what we do and why we do it. Building on the fundamental teachings of Florence Nightingale (whose views on open windows and infection control would not suit every situation and whose Victorian principles around uniform wearing have thankfully long since been eradicated), we have learnt and continue to learn. We can not only care for the sick but positively impact health promotion, wellbeing and public health, plus advocate for the patient in the interprofessional teams in which we work.

Back in 1984, I knew very little about this, and so began my lifelong lower back pain from adopting the lifting of patients from fixed height beds into armchairs. We used the Australian lift technique: this was a lift executed by two people, one on each side of the patient, who placed their shoulders under the patient's armpit to lift them. This was later banned when we realised that it put a strain on the patient's shoulders, transferred strain to the lumbar region of the nurses back and could create shear forces that damaged the patient's skin. Why was it thought okay for a 5'1" student nurse weighing 8 stone (I know, I can't believe it either!) to single-handedly support a 5'5", 12 stone patient whose stroke had resulted in a left-sided hemiplegia; moving her from the side of her bed into a chair using a rocking motion and a twisting movement? My old self can look back at my young self and ask, '*What were you thinking?*' but my young self just wanted to help Miss Hughes into the chair in time for lunch so that she could eat and watch the world go by - it made her smile in a lopsided way.

Not all learning, of course, required research to gain new skills. There was much to learn about communication from the evidence in literature, but my learning around admitting patients took place during my first couple of placements. This occurred by making errors that have remained in my consciousness, not because they caused any harm other than my own embarrassment. That adage of *'you have two ears and one mouth'* makes perfect sense as I undertook the admission process for patients. This process involves an abundance of paperwork and I, as a first-year student, went at it as a list of things to get through, leading to the writing of a plan of care. What I know now, of course, is to listen to understand, but what I did in those early days was ask all the questions and get all the answers written down. I failed to recognise that I only needed to document the information relevant to the individual patient. What I do now is to have a conversation with the patient and then document all the relevant information against my paperwork, only needing to ask questions for anything outstanding at the end.

This lesson was a painfully embarrassing one to learn as I asked Mrs Williams, who had told me in the 'past medical history' section that she had a hysterectomy five years ago, *"When was your last menstrual cycle?"* I asked Mr Jones, who only had one leg, *"Which leg are you having the knee replacement on?"*

The third situation is one, which in these days of fully understanding initial assessment scoring (Airway, Breathing, Circulation, Disability and Exposure (ABCDE)) and NEWS (National Early Warning Score) still makes me cringe. I was faced with a twenty-nine-year-old man, who was six foot tall and slim with dark curly hair. He had been admitted with a spontaneous pneumothorax (a collapse of part of his lung) and was waiting for the doctor to return to insert an underwater seal drain (chest drain to remove the air in the pleural space and allow for reinflation of the lung). I proceeded with my admission paperwork, looking for answers to my questions about his hobbies and his food likes and dislikes when I should have been encouraging him to breathe slowly, and sit forward, supported by pillows with his oxygen mask on. Thirty-six years later, I still remember he supported Everton and did not like beetroot!!

Some of the things I experienced as a young student nurse seemed melodramatic; for example, for the doctor's ward rounds, everyone was banished from the ward, with the patients all sitting bolt upright in bed and in silence. However, this did ensure that all the staff on the ward round, Consultant, Sister and a posse of junior doctors, would know everything about every patient. It also meant that the ward round book contained all the information everyone needed for the patients' continued treatment or discharge plan. I believe communication was much more effective and reliable; however, valuable learning opportunities were missed by being excluded from the ward round, except for a senior student nurse on the last placement of the three-year programme.

Making beds with those hospital corners and complete absence of creases could develop into an obsession for any of us, but, of course, linen carefully tucked in both prevents access to dust and insects (one of Florence Nightingale's directives from the war-torn hospitals that has stayed with us). Those clean, crease-free linens also help prevent pressure ulcer problems, to say nothing of comfort for the patient who had a prolonged period in bed.

During my time as a student, we were being taught to consider evidence- and research-based care. Indeed, we were the first group of students to submit a literature review as part of our final exams in my school of nursing.

One practice we reviewed at that time was related to pressure ulcers, which was the use of egg whites and oxygen to prevent further breakdown when at stage one. We would get an egg from the ward kitchen and apply the egg white to the patients' skin. Then, with them lying on their side (usually, the sacrum was the spot that we had 'egged'), a high flow oxygen mask was propped against them with the flow at fifteen litres. This practice had been undertaken for some time, and you could understand the theory behind it. The protein and oxygenation both promoted healing, and indeed it was seen to work. However, of course, that would surely be because the patient was being repositioned regularly and the pressure was being relieved from the affected areas.

We must, as a profession, ensure that we continue our progression, that we actively participate in researching our practice and share our findings widely as we all continue to learn. To ensure that changes are made in practice, the involvement of nurses in clinical roles is essential. Nurses in research and/or educational roles cannot implement the changes, nor can they evaluate them without the involvement of staff at every level and, of course, the patient.

Chapter Two

New Builds

"Great leaders do not set out to be a leader... they set out to make a difference. It is never about the role and always about the goal."

—Lisa Haisha

Within seven months of starting life as a student nurse and getting used to the environment, we were all on the move to a brand-new hospital; it was enormous. We were also the first student nurses to live in the new staff accommodation in the hospital grounds alongside the social club. Over the years, there were many evenings of fun in there with cheap drinks and loud music. Living in the nurses' home, you may as well go to the social club Thursday evening disco because no-one was going to sleep until it was all over, and those Friday early shifts meant a big breakfast in the staff canteen.

Involvement in new builds will reappear throughout my career, both working in and taking part in the commissioning of new units, but more of that later.

This new hospital in late 1984/85 brought together a general hospital and several smaller hospitals and would later include maternity and mental health services.

The experiences of this time will repeat themselves as teams are adjusted, colleagues are promoted or side lined, new role titles are introduced, leading to confusion and, at times, considerable misunderstandings about exactly who is responsible for what. This is often the case in organisational change, and local changes, along with national influences around the reorganisation of services and organisations, further compounds issues. No sooner does an organisation begin to settle into its new furrows, and then it's all change. This has left me wondering, many times over, that there could be better ways of working that would prevent such constant change. Or, at the very least, ensure that the right people lead the change to give us all the very best chance of success, to say nothing of the financial impact and waste.

Going into my second year, I was still unaware of the impact of change outside of a pristine building, a different place to live and lovely, spacious, bright, clean surroundings for patients with the most amazing views. Whilst learning about nursing was to pick up speed as we began a placement in the accident and emergency department, our social life was to expand as well. We were familiar with our local watering holes and started to venture further afield with holidays planned and excursions to other towns with music venues.

It was on one of our outings that my life was to change, and I would be spending time as a patient rather than a nurse.

As a back-seat passenger in a road traffic accident (before the days of rear seat belts being routinely fitted, never mind used), I was propelled from my seat as the car turned over, and I had neck and hand injuries. Overnight, I had gone from working in an A&E department to being a patient in one and being terrified does not begin to describe it.

"Can you feel me touching you here?" the doctor asked.

"No, where are you touching me?" is my reply as I am immobilised and stretchered to the x-ray department.

For the next 24 hours, I am nursed flat, immobile, being log-rolled, back and fore for more x-rays and given a funky pair of glasses that had a mirror on them so that I could see who was walking by or standing at the bottom of my bed. Eventually, they were to conclude that I had no bony injury to my neck; the compound dislocated fracture of my finger was reduced, and I was allowed home.

Unfortunately, as the swelling in my neck subsided, the bones moved, and the weird sensations reappeared. My return to the x-ray department was to show a subluxation of C5 & C6 (movement of, but not fractured, cervical bones in my neck) and my experience as a patient recommenced. I spent seven weeks in a Minerva plaster jacket; this was a plaster of Paris jacket that went around my head (with holes for my face and my ears) and my body, sitting on my hips. After seven weeks, the bones were still unstable, so then it was surgery, which entailed grafting bone from my pelvis into my neck. This, along with further surgery to my hand, as a tendon injury had not been repaired in the first operation, meant that I was away from work for nine long months.

During this time, I learnt a lot about the role of a nurse both in the hospital and the district nurse for ongoing wound care, and I also learnt a great deal from the patient's perspective. I am not suggesting that you need to experience things yourself to be able to care for a patient. Many of the best nurses I know have only been patients when they have had children, and many midwives have never had children, but it does not stop them from doing their job. However, I will never underestimate the impact of my experiences. It influenced my decision to work in A&E and in surgery and then in a role where I could provide one-to-one care to a patient and their family. Moreover, it made a significant difference to my view of the world and provided me with insight into the patient and family experience of healthcare, treatment and nursing care.

What do you say as a nineteen-year-old woman when feeling isolated in a hospital that is a two-hour drive from your nearest relative? And when you do have visitors for a lovely change, an elderly lady chooses that precise moment to describe her bowel habits post-operatively in great detail and at top volume! Those curtains provide no soundproofing, Mrs Thomas, and my brother (nor I, for that matter) did not need to hear, *"Nurse, it's like marbles. I need some of that medicine again."*

In turn, I was so conscious of using a bedpan whilst not allowed to sit up for five days post-op that I went into urinary retention and had to be intermittently catheterised. I was so constipated that, by the time I was allowed to go to the bathroom, I proceeded to faint on the toilet!

When I was discharged from hospital, I had low energy levels, altered body image due to scarring, a shaved head (no-one mentioned that when I signed the consent form), a slow to heal drain site at the bottom of my neck wound and a very real fear of getting in the back of a car.

As I mentioned earlier, all these experiences and emotions certainly influenced me personally but also professionally. My very real sense of the importance of empathy grew exponentially, and I really wanted to get back to work and some level of normality. It was strange to be back at my mother and stepfather's house full time for the first time in three years. That certainly curbed my student nurse lifestyle - no all-night parties here. Home was comfortable, though, and I would, later in life, appreciate how important it was for my mum to be able to look after me.

After lots of hospital appointments, scaling down of various cervical collars and physiotherapy, I was ready to return to work. However, after nine months away, it was impossible to pick up where I had left off. My group of fellow students had moved on and would very soon be third-year students, so I was introduced to my new group, and I would turn their eleven into twelve.

It was a very strange thing to recommence my placement in the A&E department with a new group of nurses. Despite the size of the new hospital, I would still have regular contact in work with my previous group indeed, I lived with three of them for a little while. My new group were nothing other than welcoming and, in fact, all except one have been lifelong friends. Thirty-six years later, I speak with them often, and we regularly have reunions. These used to consist of a meal and a night in the pub, but now we do weekends away. This is partly because we need longer to recover from the drinking, but mainly because we have so much to talk about: revisiting those early days, our own personal lives, the variety of routes our careers have taken and more recently, our retirement plans. I could never have imagined, as I tentatively got to know S684 (my new cohort that started in November 1984 – six cohorts of students per year), just how important they would be in my life. I realise I was not the first student nurse to re-join a programme of pre-registration nursing, and I certainly was not the last, but I am sure I was the luckiest.

As a group of students, we had some amazing experiences both in and out of work, and when we reminisced recently, there were some examples crying out for inclusion. Whilst we would enjoy cups of tea and custard creams after a shift, we also socialised with many a drunken night in the local pub, social club or doctors' mess, leading to some sore heads on an early shift. We recalled traction frames catching in the front of uniforms leading to us fully exposing all to everyone, and the overuse of bubbles in a bath leading to flooding and the patient shouting out, "*I'm drowning, Dr Pritchard!*" Though perhaps the funniest recollection would be insisting on taking a swab of a 'mysterious discharge' on bedding. It was keenly sent to test for culture and sensitivity in case this young man needed antibiotics - only to soon realise the 'discharge' was, in fact, fluid from an enthusiastic ejaculation!!

When I work with students now who must suspend their studies and return to a different cohort, I can empathise with them. Of course, I joined a small group; students now join a large cohort, but they are assigned to a small group within this. As I am writing this, we are still in the grip of the COVID-19 pandemic. Therefore, the vast majority of our teaching is undertaken online, whether synchronously or asynchronously (live or pre-recorded). This presents an additional barrier to students' integration into new groups. I certainly did not have that problem; indeed, we did not have mobile phones then. We had a regular queue at the payphone in the nurses' home, long before the days of FaceTime, Zoom or Teams.

It was difficult to recommence my pre-registration programme, but I did stop and consider how very different things could have been. I nursed two people, who, when they were my age, had accidents: one when diving into a shallow pool of water at a local beach, and the other, playing rugby. They were not as lucky as me, both sustaining injuries that led to them being paralysed and dependent on others for the rest of their lives. It was a total privilege to care for them, to get to know them and their families and to be able to make their frequent admissions to hospital as good an experience as was possible. I did not ever discuss my own experiences with them; however, I drew upon them frequently when planning their care with them. I believe I influenced others to adopt a more empathic approach to their care, as well as plans for rehabilitation and enhancing their limited independence.

Chapter Three

Becoming a Nurse

"Nurses are often trained to believe that they are most effective when doing for a patient. However, the essential importance of being with a patient should not be overlooked."

—Patricia Benner

I guess one of the main differences between my days as a student and current-day students (apart from the academic level of study) is that we were employed by the NHS, we were employed by the hospital, and paid a monthly salary. This meant that we were part of the established workforce. We covered shifts on the wards just like everyone else and our 'usefulness' increased as we progressed through the three years. Personally, during my first placement, I was happy to clean commodes, drip stands and beds, plus clean the pharmacy store cupboards on a Sunday afternoon shift. However, whilst these things were expected of first-years, we were also shown every aspect of care and the patient's whole experience throughout their stay on the ward.

Sometimes I worked with third-year students and most likely drove them crazy with all my questions, but they were a font of knowledge that I had to tap. Sister would work alongside students, telling us the how and the why of everything that was to be done. She sent me one day to observe a bone marrow aspiration sampling. This was undertaken at the bedside, and I was not expecting the patient to be so distressed by the procedure, so I had to leave before the end. The other patients sat me down and fetched me a glass of water - just one of many embarrassing moments until I learnt how to support the patient and not consider the impact on myself until later!

My second placement was a male medical ward; at that time, the only wards where you had male and female mixed wards, other than ITU, were trauma, emergency surgery and specialist surgery. Even on those wards, though, the patients had distinct 'ends' of the ward and separate toilets and bathrooms: very different to most hospitals now.

Anyway, on my male medical placement, we also had a series of cubicles. Haematology patients needed a single room so that they were isolated to protect them with their immunosuppression. This was my first experience with blood transfusions, and it fine-tuned my observation skills and charting skills.

These cubicles were also frequently used for private patients who were in for short periods of time. They were perfectly ordinary people who had paid to see the doctor sooner, but everyone else they saw was the same as an NHS patient. The main difference I noticed was at mealtimes when they had a silver teapot and fine china rather than the usual pots!

I was going around the ward with breakfast one morning, and as the charge nurse opened a new box of cereal, a huge dragonfly flew out! What a commotion!

"That must have been meant for the private patients; we usually have a plastic toy!" said one of the men on the ward, laughing.

Throughout this book, it is inevitable that I refer to those who I consider as role models: some in a positive manner and others less so. The first two ward Sisters and their deputies worked alongside the rest of the team; they looked after students and made sure we were okay whilst at the same time they expected us to work hard and hold our own. Many a time, I would be sent home from a morning shift at 1.00 pm, walk back to the nurse's home and then return to the ward at 5.00 pm to work the rest of the late shift. I am not sure how well received this arrangement would be now, but we needed to cover both shifts, and respectfully, I took my turn to do this.

My third ward Sister, in the new hospital, was formidable; this working relationship was built more upon fear than it was on respect. She stopped me one day in the middle of the ward, took my hat off, pinned my ponytail into a bun on the back of my head and pinned my hat back in place, all without uttering a single word. The message was clear, and I have always been strict about the wearing of our uniform, dress code, jewellery etc. However, I hope that I positively role model that by example rather than by fear and force.

When I returned to the programme after my accident, I completed my placement in A&E. It was an extraordinary environment that influenced my later career greatly. Then allocated to a specialist surgical placement, I avoided eyes and ENT, phew, and off I went to gynaecology. What an amazing ward Sister I was to meet there. She ran that ward with such precision and organisation that, even on the busiest theatre days, everything went like clockwork. This experience probably made me the surgical nurse that I was to become. Understanding the pre- and post-operative care of patients was impossible to avoid as she made sure that I could explain why we did everything we did, and I was fascinated. This was the placement where I learnt how to catheterise, and indeed, by the end of ten weeks, I could almost insert a urinary catheter with my eyes closed.

The emotional impact was different from my other placements. It was challenging to care for patients who had had a spontaneous abortion (usually called a miscarriage), whilst also caring for patients who had been admitted to have a planned termination of their pregnancy (an abortion). This dichotomy was perplexing; however, both women needed nursing care, and it was our role to provide this.

It was on this ward that I learnt a valuable lesson about perception. The family of a patient and the ward staff perceived that withholding information from a patient was protecting her; however, her view was that we had lied to her. It caused me to really explore the ethics around whose information this was anyway. So, this very lovely lady had gone for surgery and returned to the ward, not having undergone the expected procedure. The surgeon found an advanced cancerous tumour and evidence of spread and so 'closed the patient up' and sent her back to the ward. We were under strict instructions not to tell her anything because, when the surgeon spoke to the family, that was what they wanted. I had real difficulty caring for her with that elephant in the room; surely she knew. Indeed, one day, she confronted her family, who told her the truth.

Later, when I tried to help her to the toilet, she said, *"Leave me alone. I liked you, I trusted you, but you lied to me."*

It was several days later when she called me over to apologise, and we hugged and cried together. Whilst provision of information has changed beyond all recognition from this time, the whole experience has never left me, and this lady taught me a lot about compassion.

A few days before the end of this placement, I cared for a lady who was in receipt of palliative care for a similar sort of tumour. She had very few visitors, and Sister expected someone to sit with this lady when her family were not there. I took my turn and indeed volunteered to sit with her, holding her hand, reading her book to her and just sitting quietly as she waited for the latest dose of analgesia to take effect. This lady was to be the first person that I was to sit alone with as she drew her last breath.

29

What a privilege it is to be a nurse and to share such private moments with people.

The role modelling continued as the Sister asked me to show her how we were to undertake the first and last offices, comfort the family when they arrived and complete all the paperwork. How pleased was I that I knew to talk to my patient as if she was still here, open the window a little and maintain dignity and respect to the very last moment?

Moving into the second year of my course, I was to be taken away from acute general nursing to a Learning Disability placement; this was an essential part of our programme for adult nurses to experience learning disability or mental health nursing as well as a placement in midwifery and paediatrics.

The NMC standard at that time allowed more clinical hours and less taught theory. Therefore, after six weeks in the school of nursing, the programme progressed with six to ten weeks of placement, one week of school, one- or two-weeks' leave, one week of school and then off to placement again. The three years flew by.

The learning disability placement was hospital-based and had many challenges. Firstly, finding my way around; secondly, understanding who the staff were and who the residents were; thirdly, trying to understand what possible use I could be in what appeared to be a chaotic and confused environment. Like all placements, it takes a little while to settle in, but by the end of ten weeks, I was convinced that once qualified, I would then train to be a learning disability nurse. I loved caring for and working with these people. There was so much I could do, from sitting back and letting the residents do things independently; identifying physical health issues and problems with medication that helped the residents and the nurses; taking two of the older residents, who had spent most of their lives living here, out for day trips to the seaside and a treat in the café on the promenade.

There were some scary moments in this placement as some residents could be inexplicably violent. I usually managed to 'dodge the bullet,' but on one occasion, I took a real knock to my head. The learning from this placement has stayed with me and is probably more pertinent now in my personal life and in society, as well as professionally. It is about accepting difference, recognising people who live with autism or ADHD or Downs, for example, and appreciating their view of the world. Knowing, as people in general, and as nurses in particular, we must pay attention to our own attitudes and behaviours and ensure that we consider each person as an individual. This is paramount to plan and attain person-centred care successfully.

Following on from my time in the learning disability placement, I was to go out in the community, spending time with a district nurse and a health visitor. The care provided in patients' homes has never ceased to amaze me. As a student nurse, I learnt so much about observation skills, taking things in quickly to ensure everyone was safe and also assessing the issues the patient may be experiencing in their home. Often the reason for a referral to the district nurse, health visitor or the scheduled visit was the tip of the iceberg, and what was required was more complex than anticipated.

The district nurse taught me so much about observation when it came to the environment of care that many of my initial thoughts about care, based on a hospital setting, were challenged. Who knew you could clean and redress a wound aseptically without a dressing trolley? You just need to get the pets out of the room, persuade the patient not to touch anything and precariously balance dressing packs on coffee tables, footstools and chair arms. I also learnt a thing or two about bandaging and injections - skills to stand me in good stead forever.

I had the opportunity to visit patients across the lifespan with the health visitor. I visited many homes, some in affluent areas, some in poor areas, some with three generations living in close quarters; this experience was to help with my understanding of society, culture and difference.

One eye-opening visit was to a new mother and her baby on a traveller's site. At first sight, it was chaotic with children and dogs running wild, playing in mud and dirt, open fires, scary stares from men standing in small groups, smoking, talking quietly and then shouting at the children. I really did not want to get out of the car, but when we did, everybody was polite and respectful. I inside of the shiny, metal caravan was spotless, not a whiff of smoke, quiet and calm with a beautiful baby dressed in wool and lace. I am not sure if I have ever experienced such a battering of my senses but a terrific insight into how differently people live within our diverse society.

"Who wants to work on Christmas day?"

"ME, ME," said no-one ever!

We were on our paediatric placement for Christmas, and between us, we were covering Christmas Eve, Christmas Day and Boxing Day - or at least that was the planned roster. As it happened, whilst the hospital worked hard to discharge as many patients as possible by Christmas and close wards as we had so many empty beds (a phenomenon no longer experienced at any time of year), an influx of admissions to the paediatric ward with norovirus led to a rapid spread throughout the staff. Those who made it into the morning shift on Christmas Eve were not seen again for three days as they succumbed, closely followed by all of us who lived in the nurse's home. Staffing on the ward was depleted with sick registrants and sick students, and the nurse's home was not a happy Christmas environment – wretched, utterly wretched.

Once paediatrics was over (not an area I ever imagined returning to, I love children, but sick children, a ward full of them, was not for me), next was a ten-week stint of night shifts. My placement was a surgical ward, and we were rostered to work two nights on, two nights off, ten nights on (yes, TEN nights in a row!), ten nights off! The placement absolutely flew by, and I learnt that after working all night, my feet were burning, I was starving hungry, and I was capable of sleep that no-one could wake me from - no 'do not disturb' sign required.

The night shifts were busy in the week and always especially so on a Tuesday and Wednesday night when we had six to eight patients post TURP (transurethral resection of the prostate). What skills I gained, along with muscles, from hanging bags of irrigation fluid and 'milking' catheter tubing all night to ensure that blood and urine drained without blocking and that the fluid balance charts balanced beautifully by handover in the morning. Caring for these post-operative patients was a steep learning curve, but it was also incredibly rewarding. They were all men in their 60s or 70s, and they were pleased to have the surgery that promised to relieve their symptoms. They were respectful to the nurses, and they all seemed to have a superb sense of humour with a hint of wickedness, an example of which I will set the scene for now.

Students on nights worked on a ward with one other student and health care support workers. So, most nights, we had 28 patients, two second-year student nurses and two HCSWs. We worked well together, split the ward in two and worked hard all night long. Weekends could be a little quieter with no elective surgery, several empty beds and some patients almost ready for discharge home; a few even taking it in turns to take the bedtime drinks trolley around the ward. It was in these quieter times that the night Sister would come along to prepare us students for our medicines assessment.

Routinely, the night Sister would visit the ward in the night and the morning to undertake the medicines round, and the doctor would come along to administer any intravenous medicines. During our night shift placement, we were to undertake our medicines assessment, and each and every one of us were terrified. We tested each other on the BNF and the medicines policy and procedure, but nothing could really prepare us for the interrogation we were going to experience. Now clearly, medicines management is critical to safe patient care, so the importance of knowledge cannot be underestimated, but the fear of the night Sister really turned up the pressure. The night Sister would expect you to be able to take her around the ward and tell her all about every patient, no notes to refer to, just depend upon your memory, and thankfully, my memory then was much sharper than it might be now. As you moved from patient to patient, you would prepare and administer all the oral medicines, and she might ask you any number of questions about any one of them. We all knew this was coming; we had studied hard and, as I mentioned, tested one another in an attempt to know everything about all our patients and all the medicines that we would be giving to them.

The night Sister was not a cruel person; indeed, she was friendly; however, she was very strict. You were not going to pass this assessment if you could not answer her questions and demonstrate safe and efficient medicine administration.

Well, so she came along to assess me on a weekend shift. We had worked our way through most of the ward and entered the last four-bedded bay of post-operative TURP patients who were all 4- or 5-days post-op and feeling quite well; they would be going home in a couple of days. They had got to know one another pre- and post-op and recovered enough to become amused by the staff and often quite cheeky. One of the four patients was blind and was also the most mischievous. The night Sister had quite a gruff, and certainly loud, voice (quite the opposite of me).

As I approached this patient gently to avoid startling him, she called out, *"Mr Jones, sit up properly now to take your tablets."*

His response was, *"By God, who is that? Old Nick?!"* (The devil.)

The rest of the patients laughed; I almost died on the spot as I explained to him what was happening, and Sister was looking quite cross. How I continued, I am not sure, but the night Sister passed my assessment and praised my confidence in dealing with my patients. As I went around the ward later, turning off the lights, I said to Mr Jones, *"My goodness, you almost made me choke earlier. Did you not realise who she was?"*

"Oh, Nurse, bach, I knew alright - how much fun do you think blind men have, eh?"

Bach translates from Welsh to English as 'small' - it is used in this situation as a term of endearment - like 'little one'.

Chapter Four

Being a Student

"Leadership is not about being in charge. Leadership is about taking care of those in your charge."

—Simon Sinek

I mentioned earlier that working with senior students was an excellent way to learn, but, in some ways, it was also scary; how would I ever be like them? I guess we all must feel like that at some time, and indeed there are some colleagues in my current place of work who have that same effect on me.

Of course, I did not imagine someone would look at me and wonder, but as I have gained knowledge and skills through my own development and experience, I understand it is the natural course of things.

As a second-year student, I supported the 'new ones,' and then when I was a third-year, I was able to teach and support the practices of other students and gain supervisory and delegation skills. This experience was to be the foundation of both my management skills and my role as a teacher and an assessor.

I think as the preparation of pre-registration undergraduate nurses changed, many registrants lost sight of their importance in the mentoring, teaching and assessment of students. I believe there was something about students no longer being employed by a hospital-based school of nursing that translated into them being seen as university students. Well, of course, they are university students who are governed by university policies and procedures. However, if nurses in placement areas do not view the students as 'belonging,' then they will not feel like part of the team. There is a chance that registrants may lose sight of their responsibility for the development of our future nurses. Of course, the new Education Standards (NMC, 2018) should contribute greatly to gaining a sense of belonging for both students and registrants. As Academic Assessors, we are to be instrumental in ever-improving the experience for students and their supervisors/ assessors in practice. The learning and assessment of the future nurse remain 50% in practice and 50% in theory, so the students 'belong' to the university **and** to practice.

In response to COVID-19, the emergency education standards removed some students temporarily from practice placements. However, those who remained in practice experienced placements where they worked increasingly alongside students from other stages in the programme. This enriched their experiences and was helpful in understanding the development of students throughout the programme.

Thinking back to my days as a student nurse, we took on responsibilities, especially on night shifts, that we might consider now were perhaps outside of our scope. We were supervised by night Sisters and Matrons who seemed to have a propensity to know everything about everything.

I enjoyed every one of my placements, and at the end of them all (except midwifery and paediatrics), I vowed that was the place I would return to as a staff nurse - I loved it all. Ultimately, though, trauma and orthopaedics won through, and my journey to critical care nursing began in earnest.

My student experiences ensured I was respectful of all areas of nursing. Each and every one was fascinating, plus I walked away with the desire to continue learning and to share with others at every single opportunity.

Chapter Five

Relationships

"*Excellence requires commitment and involvement, but it also requires power. Since caring is central to nursing, then power without excellence is an anathema.*"

—Patricia Benner

When I first set out as a student nurse, everyone was addressed by their title, and no-one used Christian names on the wards. It was probably in the late 80s/early 90s that this started to change, but there was still a certain reverence about people considered to be senior and/or powerful. This continues to be the case now with many doctors but is certainly not true with nurses, other disciplines or senior managers. In some respects, it all seems friendlier; however, I would suggest that once established as a manager, it is not your role to be everyone's friend as this can make it very difficult to do the job at hand.

As a manager, I was always content to be addressed by my name when in the office or a meeting, but I preferred titles to be used in the clinical area. It seems to me, rightly or wrongly, that this provides a professional image, and it also prevents wasting precious time with small talk. When addressing me as Sister, everyone seemed to get to the point immediately, and I could respond to their questions or requests promptly too. It has never been my intention that I should be scary, or people are fearful. It was, and remains, my intention to build working relationships in a professional and respectful manner.

Gaining an understanding of the roles of others is imperative in ensuring successful interprofessional working. It is not enough to be a multi-disciplinary team (MDT). We must be able to work together and deliver the best possible care and services in our NHS and not merely stand in our own corner in an MDT to get 'what we need.' I have made lifelong friends with colleagues from across all professional groups as well as from all fields of nursing and many healthcare providers and partners. It is this deep understanding of what others do that enables relationship building, which makes it a pleasure when we succeed.

No-one can get along with everyone, and hence there have been times when working relationships have been tested, strained and found wanting. By far, my biggest difficulty throughout my career was one relatively short period of time (though it was intense and felt a lot longer than it was) when working with a group of surgeons.

Right away, I must emphasise that there is no generalisation here and that I have had an amazingly positive working relationship with many doctors, anaesthetists and, indeed, surgeons. However, this particular small group caused me some serious issues and tested my professionalism to its very limits.

It really is quite easy to deal with all manner of issues and differences when you can provide a sound rationale that is backed up by research and demonstrated by best practice via a calm and reasonable discussion. Unfortunately, when a person is unreasonable, will not provide a rationale, want things done 'their way' and then shifts to an approach that becomes a personal affront, you are in a whole new realm of an autocratic approach. These behaviours brought out a defiance in me that was fuelled simply by the immorality of the approach to staff, whose only driver was to do the right thing for their patients. During this period of time, my home and work life blurred around the edges. I received frequent telephone calls during my time off over difficult situations for staff when confronted with often unreasonable behaviour of some of our colleagues.

I am not proud that on two occasions, I swore at my surgical colleagues, but their behaviour was bizarre, rude and intimidating, and my cool was momentarily lost! There were many more difficult conversations that did not result in bad language but did lead to me feeling frustrated with their general attitudes towards everyone else in the team and to me in particular. I fought long and hard to ensure the highest standards of care and advancing practice, but ultimately, the power of the surgical team made it impossible for me to remain. So, when a role came up that appealed to me, I consciously walked away. One of the surgeons came to see me in my office and asked me, *"How can you leave now, Louise, when your staff all support you? You have won battles, but the war remains!"*

It was clear to me that my decision to leave was the right one as I never signed up to fight a war.

Patients, of course, are, in the main, unquestioning and will simply accept the explanations provided to them, especially when given by medical staff. To hear and to read about how 'incredible' the surgeons are and how 'they saved my life' is okay; however, no-one cares single-handedly. Whilst surgeons' skills are utterly amazing - holding a brain or a heart in their hands - every aspect of care is utterly incredible, from birth to death. The privilege of being involved at every single stage is mind-blowingly astonishing. Without every single person's piece of the jigsaw, we would never succeed.

Of course, when a patient is told, *"This is a huge and complicated operation, and you may be on intensive care for weeks afterwards,"* yet the next day they are sat in a chair eating breakfast, patients may believe their surgeon is a miracle worker. Whereas, of course, their recovery is down to many more things than one surgeon.

I do not want you to imagine that relationships are always difficult between medics and nurses because that is not the case. I have many nurse/doctor friends who are very happy as couples, never mind happy to work very well together. Indeed, in-between colleagues in every professional group there will be differences, which is to be expected with so many of us working together. I do believe the increase in all genders being recognised as successful in every professional group should help make a real difference to working relationships. I am a firm believer in the growing number of male nurses helping reduce the bitchiness that could develop within a group of mainly female nurses. Why shouldn't the nursing profession be open to all? It makes us better.

So, I have witnessed the breakdown of working relationships within medical teams, and, in my experience, this has been less in relation to personalities and more about conceit, pride and greed. The drivers of private healthcare or NHS monies paid for additional work has been like fuel on an open fire, breaking teams and causing investigations into how these teams might work together again. Allegations and counter-allegations about these behaviours within the medical staff are not my information to share. However, their behaviour had an impact on many staff from several professional groups and left me to ask why are we here?

I know that I did not go to work in the NHS for any other reason than to be a part of the most amazing organisation in the world. I remain horrified at those who work in it and ask, 'What's in it for me?' Well, apart from your monthly salary, there is nothing in it for you, other than knowing the privilege that it is to care for others.

It would be naïve to imagine that working in the services that the NHS provides will not take its toll on the majority of people at one time or another. With this in mind, I was interested to learn about Schwartz Centre Rounds® and how these could support all staff with the emotional toll of working within healthcare. These Rounds were open to all and any staff and presented an opportunity to listen to the stories of others and then describe how they might resonate with you and how you feel about episodes of care or about the work that you do. They are not forums to problem solve or advise, but rather a platform to gain an understanding of the roles of others and the emotional impact of their work.

These Rounds provided me with the opportunity to increase my knowledge of the roles of staff from every area of healthcare. I met literally hundreds of people that I would never have met otherwise. The forums enriched my understanding of how others define care and how it makes them feel. I listened to administrative and secretarial staff, CEO's and other executive board members, therapy staff, technical staff, porters, domestics, pastoral team, surgeons, anaesthetists, physicians, psychiatrists, nurses from every field, managers and psychologists. The experience heartened me, as did seeing tears of sadness and joy and the support openly offered enabled staff to continue working in their roles when they had felt they could or should not.

Schwartz Rounds® allowed me to recognise that without open communication and a true understanding of one another, teams really do not stand a chance of survival. We simply become groups of people working in the same place.

The other essential ingredient for teamwork is recognition of one another's strengths - and not just knowing it but naming it. I have often struggled with accepting compliments or praise; it's far easier to be self-deprecating than to be graceful in acceptance and enjoy success. Indeed, when patients thank nurses, you will often hear, *"That's no problem; it's my job."* In the main, patients are thanking us for the way we do things as opposed to the act that is our job. The way we do things is what patients will remember, and it is this that they thank us for. It took me a long time to change my response to *"You are very welcome."* When patients say, *"I'm sorry for being so much trouble, nurse,"* then *"Not at all; it is my pleasure to help you,"* displays our desire to care far more than saying, *"It's what I'm paid for."*

I do sometimes still struggle when patients, families or colleagues tell me that I am good at what I do. When I provide positive feedback to others, I really want them to recognise their strengths and enjoy the praise. I discourage any self-deprecation and seek their acknowledgement and recognition of just how good they are. If I am to role model that behaviour, I must also accept praise in a gracious manner. So, when two colleagues recently said to me, *"Do you know how good you are?"* just before I jumped in with denial, I corrected myself and said, *"Thank you both. That is very kind."* It actually felt very nice indeed.

Chapter Six

Experiences as a Staff Nurse

"Integrity is doing the right thing even when no-one is watching."

—CS. Lewis

At the point of qualifying in 1988, I was interviewed for a staff nurse post. At the interview, I was clear that I wanted to work on one of the orthopaedic wards or any other surgical ward. There were enough jobs for all the nurses qualifying, but of course, not everyone would have their job of choice.

"Well, Nurse Giles, what will you do if we offer you a job in theatre?"

This was not at all what I wanted, but I could hardly believe it when I said, *"Offer me a job in theatre, and I'll tell you then."*

I'm not sure who was the most surprised, and remarkably, they gave me a post on the ward that was my first choice! So, off I went with my blue epilates, blue stripe on my hat and my shiny silver belt buckle to a twenty-three-bed orthopaedic ward with elective work and transfers from the trauma ward, a mixed ward with adults of all ages.

Within two weeks of starting on the ward, I was left in charge on an afternoon shift. With a student nurse and a HCSW, I quickly learnt the art of teamwork and safe delegation, plus how to walk very quickly back and fore to theatre to collect patients. This first job provided the opportunity to consolidate much of my learning about pre- and post-operative care, wound care and medicines. All staff nurses were required to call on the Matron, Ward Sister or Doctor when it came to intravenous medicines or fluids or controlled drugs, though this was to change rapidly in the coming year or so.

I grasped the opportunity at this early stage to gain insight into the management of the ward, and duty rotas were, strangely, one of my favourite things. As a student, I had seen many different approaches and levels of both generosity and selfishness. One of my first experiences of positive role modelling, in relation to rosters, was from the Sister on the gynaecology ward, who influenced my approach. Duty rotas are now generated using a computer programme, but without the human touch and a fair and equitable approach, I believe the impact on staff morale and retention is damaging.

Whilst during my pre-registration programme, I worked with senior students, and then, of course, I took my turn to work with junior students. It was as a newly qualified nurse that I was to work with students and learn much about supervision, teaching and assessment. As individuals, we naturally apply the important principles of mentorship and role modelling and always aim to do so in a positive way. However, this is not always straightforward. After all this time, I can still vividly recall having to provide constructive, critical feedback to a student nurse whose behaviour with some of the younger patients was less than professional. I could relate to the difficulties she experienced as those patients were the same age as her. I was only three years older but felt like a parent chastising a child. Little was I to know that I would experience this feeling many times over my career; indeed, my maternal tendencies are still required occasionally.

As we often worked on the wards with only one registrant, it was not at all unusual to seek advice/information from the registrant on one of the neighbouring wards. It was on one of these sojourns that I became involved with my first ever cardiac arrest. Many of my colleagues had witnessed such events during their pre-registration days, but not me. How remarkable that all that training, practice and updates came through and enabled me to recognise what was happening, shout for help and commence resuscitation until the team arrived. It is a situation that I have seen many, many times since, but the sense of responsibility fired with the aftereffects of adrenaline when the emergency has passed never alters whether the outcome for the patient is positive or not.

At almost twelve months post-registration, my friend and I decided we would go and work somewhere else to gain experience with a plan to return after a year. We thought it would be good for us to work in a different hospital, and undoubtedly it did not do us any harm. Over thirty years on, I have worked in five different hospitals but have never returned to my original one. This was not a conscious decision, but life has just taken me along different roads.

My next post as a staff nurse was to be the start of my somewhat obsessive critical care pathway, general ITU first. Not a place that I had experienced for more than a few shifts as a student, but nonetheless, it was an area of patient care that I rapidly became fascinated by. I was fortunate to start working there at the same time as a few others. We supported one another, ensuring our survival through some tough times when caring for tragic cases and enjoying one another's company on a social basis. It is so very important that we look out for one another, which is sometimes professionally through clinical supervision, sometimes personally via coffee and a chat, or sometimes letting our hair down in a more sociable and occasionally alcohol-influenced setting.

My learning in ITU was swift. There was so much to learn and the need to apply that learning so quickly. Before I knew what was happening, I was supporting others in their early days in the department. I cared for adults who were elective post-operative admissions as well as emergency medical, surgical and trauma patients. Everyone I worked with, from every professional group, were keen to teach, and I have never forgotten that. I have always been happy to share my own knowledge and acknowledge when I don't know something. This is the time to send the student away to find out, but come back and tell me once they know. No-one knows it all, and these days, I don't always remember everything that I do know!

In this job, I also experienced both positive and negative role modelling that has influenced my own attitude and leadership. As people caring for people, our roles as nurses can be draining on our emotions as well as on us physically. It is fair to say that we can make mistakes; however, this is part of being human. Whilst in my career, I have made two medicines errors: neither harming the patient, but both seriously denting my confidence and my pride. It is imperative that we are not complacent when undertaking things that we have done many times before. Even with the very best intentions, as humans, we will get things wrong sometimes. How important is it that we know that these errors are handled fairly, properly and in a way that prevents future mistakes? It is vital that this is the case if we are to learn from our practice.

My first medication error took place on a night shift in ITU. I was caring for a patient who was being nursed in isolation; he was very sick indeed and not expected to survive. My error was to administer one of his intravenous medicines in a solution of 10mls and not 100mls. I spotted my error when totalling up the fluid balance chart several hours later.

The doctor's response was, *"Don't worry, Louise. This has not harmed the patient at all; I'll document it in the notes."*

Of course, I reported my error to the nurse in charge and then had to wait for the manager in the morning to be 'told off.' As I mentioned earlier, whilst adhering to the appropriate policies, I would always approach this type of situation in a supportive manner, considering why this happened and if there was something about the process that could address the human factors associated with this type of error. Unfortunately, my experience was far more punitive and left me feeling low in confidence and unable to sleep properly - potentially a recipe for disaster when I returned to work the next night.

There is much to be learnt from how people make you feel. When I made my second drug error, it was some twenty years later, and I self-reported it. The patient came to no harm and my manager tried to 'tell me off;' however, this time, I explained to her that I felt terrible about what had happened. I illustrated why the error had occurred, and I presented a change in practice that would prevent this error from ever happening again. The outcome was so much more positive, everything was reported as per policy, but I knew that my error influenced a change in practice that reduced risk dramatically. That is why we should not only apply policy but also learn from any mistakes made so that we may positively influence practice and patient care.

In my role in ITU, I also cared for children. Learning to care safely for a child who is ventilated was a totally new experience and one which has influenced me and remained with me throughout my career. Three children stay with me clearly; one was ventilated after a severe episode of asthma; this child became unwell so quickly; however, she recovered rapidly as well; it was a joy to see for us as a team and, of course, for her and her family.

Another child I cared for was a much sadder case, and she was not to recover. She did not live long enough to celebrate her first birthday, and this was an absolute tragedy for the family.

I had been with them through the last few hours of her life, and almost all the rapport building and care were undone when Sister came in and said, *"We will be taking her to the mortuary now."*

The horror in their faces mirrored my own as I quickly stepped in to undo the damage.

"I will take her to the Chapel of Rest. I will carry her there with the porter, and you will be able to arrange to come in and see her tomorrow."

The family were grateful, and I hope they completely forgot Sister's faux pas, but I have never forgotten and always been careful of how we word things sensitively. Our words can be so very powerful.

My third and fondly remembered child patient was a little one who was admitted with meningococcal meningitis; he was a much-loved boy with a family who were dedicated to him. I can remember distinctly caring for him day after day, often with a new ITU nurse who was keen to learn and his parents sitting intently in the cubicle with us. He was desperately unwell, and whilst he survived, his future was to be influenced by mobility issues and respiratory problems but nonetheless loved by his family. One day, whilst teaching a new nurse about his care, another colleague came in for handover for the next shift.

She was chatting with the patient's mother as I finished teaching, and she told my colleague, *"Louise is proper Sister material."*

All these years on, my colleague still teases me when I see her.

Receiving feedback from families and patients should never be underestimated. They see things we might not see, and they are usually totally comfortable in saying out loud what others may only think, whether positive or not! The building of relationships is paramount in every aspect of nursing. The rewards are potentially enormous, whether they be about the team we work with, our self-awareness and self-esteem or the learning that takes place and influences us as leaders. When building relationships, we sometimes have to break down barriers. This was quite literally the case when I was, back in October 1990, caring for a young man who was visiting the UK. He was from Germany, and that afternoon shift, we watched together the breaking down of the Berlin Wall on the BBC news. The conversations with that patient about relationships and barriers were truly profound.

My next place of work, on my self-imposed rotational programme, took me to the accident and emergency department. I had experienced A&E as a student nurse and as a patient, and now, as a staff nurse, I was to draw upon all my learning and my experience as an orthopaedic nurse and an ITU nurse. I stayed working in A&E for four years, and it shaped me both as a professional and also personally. I met so many students I have had the pleasure of working with in other areas in the NHS and, indeed, now, in the university. I also made lifelong friends during this time who have been influential on my practice and my personal life.

Some of the people I looked after in the A&E department presented with very ordinary issues: a sprained ankle, a bump to the head, small lacerations etc., etc. Medical emergencies presented patients with heart attacks, strokes, respiratory problems and, of course, sporting injuries, most especially from rugby injuries on a Saturday afternoon.

I learnt a lot about the care of a multitude of patients and developed my knowledge and skills in the management of trauma patients. This department saw many tragic things with the loss of patients from all age groups and all ethnicities. This often-presented challenges when accommodating cultural differences when there is a sudden and unexpected death.

For example, caring for a young girl who died from a terrible accident, that caused fatal head injuries. Also, caring for that girl's parents as well after such a shock, making sure they knew that everyone had done everything possible, but there was no recovery from her injuries.

Caring for a teenage girl with significant injuries from an RTA was challenging as it had been a traumatic scene for the paramedic team, and she would learn later that some of her friends had not survived. I worked with a student nurse on this day, and after transferring our patient to ITU and tidying up together, she said to me, *"If I am, one day, half as good as you, I will be happy."* To realise that the care you provide can influence another nurse in such a positive way is incredibly uplifting and another good reason to enjoy working side by side with a student nurse. One day she may care for me or one of mine.

Of course, A&E was not all high drama. We could, in those days, have some shifts, particularly on weekday nights, that when we cleared the department, there was only so much cleaning and restocking we could do before getting up to mischief. A good sign of a great team was that we could laugh at and with one another and always be aware there could be a trick around the corner. Some of my colleagues were fabulous actors and could lead a junior doctor a merry dance before they realised they were being taken for a ride. Hiding in cupboards and jumping out can cause a riot in the middle of the night, but we need to keep ourselves entertained as there is only so much tea you can drink! Now, of course, there does not seem to be any downtime, but even if there is only five minutes, filling it with laughter lifts the spirits and makes the tragedies easier to cope with.

Away from work, the team spirit continued with infamous fundraising annual discos, fundraising balls, BBQs at the consultant's house and the hospital show. The A&E department could always be found treading the boards, acting out and providing their take on a song; nurses and doctors galore causing riotous laughter and tears of joy and embarrassment. What on earth would get me to pose in a waiting room scene in a raincoat with a tennis racquet protruding from my rear!?!

As well as the shenanigans influencing me, my passion for teaching was further developed when working in A&E. During quiet spells, we would set up scenarios to run through many eventualities so that students and new members of staff could get a feel for situations before experiencing them for real. Trauma cases were my 'favourite,' and burn injuries were to become my next fascination. I applied to work in the next new build to come to the hospital and return to an intensive care setting, more specialised than the previous one but drawing on all my energies, knowledge, patience, leadership and skills.

Chapter Seven

More Experiences

Back in an ITU setting, caring for adults and children was mostly a fabulous opportunity, even when caring for patients who were not going to survive. I met a number of like-minded, passionate, accomplished and dedicated nurses in that place. The opportunity to work with them, as well as surgeons, anaesthetists and physiotherapists, added immeasurably to my own development.

I became totally aware of my role as the patients' advocate but also drew upon my experiences of exemplary leadership and solid management at previous workplaces, and I worked hard to instil these approaches in others.

It was whilst working here that I formally applied reflective practice leading to an additional qualification, as well as my first publication. It took place on a night shift caring for a patient who was so badly injured from burns that they were barely recognisable as a person. It was simply the worst injury that any of us present had ever seen and, when the patient inevitably died, within an hour of arrival, it was for me to support the nursing team and take a staff nurse with me to speak with the family. This was to support the staff nurse's development as she would soon apply for a more senior post and would be in a role like mine. Therefore, she needed experience in being the patient's advocate in ensuring a dignified death; being a teacher, a role model, and an advocate for the family were skills she required.

When talking with the family and comforting them in their loss and their grief, I knew they would ask to see their relative. I did not want to tell them that they could not, but knowing that they had been present at the scene, I thought they would appreciate that it might be better for them to remember their relative as was before this terrible accident rather than after our medical interventions and the burn injuries.

My published reflective piece was about recognising how influential nurses can be and how important it is to consider the people concerned and not influence their decisions based on your personal view of the situation. With all the facts and after listening to the family talking about their loss, I acted purely with kindness, and I am resolute that it was the right thing to do for them.

My next move, to another new build, involved working in Oxford for six months to gain experience and insight prior to the cardiac unit opening. This unit was the one in which I gained my treasured Sisters post. I talk elsewhere in the book about the challenges in the unit with relationships, excellent teamwork and development and succession planning. Here, I want to explore the impact of 'just knowing' - that intuitive practice that leads to clinical decision making that may not seem rational to others, but sometimes you 'just know.'

One situation was caring for a patient post-operatively who was a good deal younger than our usual patients. It was a post-operative recovery that ought to have been straightforward, and that did happen, but not immediately. The patient was settled into the ITU bed, and the staff nurse was in control. She was teaching her student about all the right, colourful wavy lines on the monitor, with everything looking fine, but I just knew something was wrong. Within moments, we were resuscitating that patient, and the surgeon had to take another look inside the patient's chest. These complications happen sometimes, but we picked up on it so quickly that within an hour, the patient was settled again. Anyone who had walked off for an hour and then returned would not know anything had happened.

The student nurse who had enjoyed her placement told me she would not be applying for a job as she could not contemplate knowing how to respond to such an emergency. Well, no, of course, she could not, neither would I in her shoes. However, experience, knowledge and skills put us in the right place.

The next morning, when I made that patient a cup of tea, they turned to me and said, *"You make awful tea."*

I can save lives but make tea? Clearly not!

Chapter Eight

Role Modelling

"Be who you are and say what you feel, because those who mind do not matter and those who matter do not mind."

—Dr Seuss

I have mentioned role modelling at other points, but I want to emphasise how powerful our behaviour and approach can be on others. You hear people talking about *'talking the talk'* and *'walking the walk,'* but for me, it is so simple - **lead by example**.

With this in mind, you certainly do not need to be the most senior person in the team/department/hospital/organisation to lead by example as we can all learn from others, and their role should not be seen as the most important thing. For me, it is more about what they say/do/present themselves and then, of course, the impact of their actions on the patient/team/service/organisation.

As a student nurse, I worked with some very strict nurses who, at times, were a little scary in as much as you would not want to do anything wrong. I did not ever want to be a nurse that instilled fear – rather, I want others to respect me, and I will respect them. Respect comes from everyone recognising that you are credible in your role. You are capable; you will look for the guidance of others when coming up against something new;

you will ensure you keep yourself up to date; you will encourage and empower others, and you can be trusted to be honest and fair. These are qualities that are so very important to me and, I believe, so very important in nursing and, indeed, for all health care staff.

Some of the role models who have influenced my development and my practice over the years range from senior professional staff from nursing, medicine, physiotherapy, speech and language, psychology, dental nursing and pharmacy, as well as technical staff. Some of these people have moved into senior positions in the NHS and to head up nursing, in particular, in other organisations across the country. Some are my colleagues in practice on the same level as me (and they know who they are), and others have helped me grow in my role as an educator. There are those who, if we must categorise people, do not sit in professional teams; however, they are leaders in a way that perhaps they do not really recognise. Their impact on me when considering ways to include everyone, the language we use and building respectful relationships cannot be overestimated.

One example of a language change that made a massive impact was when senior staff from our education commissioners were presenting to a HCSW Conference. One speaker talked about the development of 'unqualified staff,' and after about ten minutes or so, one of the HCSWs put up her hand.

"Excuse me, but I object to being referred to as unqualified. I hold several qualifications that I have worked hard to achieve and so that I might undertake my role in the team. I think what you mean to say is non-registrant."

I had always been aware of this, but from that day forward, I was determined to correct anyone that used qualified/unqualified rather than using registrant/non-registrant. If one person can speak up in an auditorium and challenge the use of language (to riotous applause, I might add!), we can surely all do the same, especially as this particular phraseology applies to so many staff groups.

I think that the one thing that I have in common with everyone who has been a positive role model for me is the fact that we are all concerned with the patient being the centre of all that we do.

"Just remember to keep the important thing as the important thing."

This is something that I can hear one of my role models saying as I write it down; he was inspirational to me when he was working clinically, in education, in leadership, and even when he was a patient. All those nurses, and other staff, who have/are positive role models for me would never lose sight of the important thing.

Unfortunately, there are a number of people that I have encountered over the years, at varying levels in organisations, whose focus is not on the *'important thing'* but on *'What's in it for me?'*

You will recognise these people if you take the time to reflect as they are not true team players. They will gladly take the credit for positive outcomes and just as readily look to apportion blame when something goes wrong. My experience of negative role models is that they are not to be relied upon. They are not always supportive, may well bend the truth to suit their ends, and on top of that, do not treat others fairly and equitably. This looks like a dark picture, yet it is a true picture. Still, it must be said that I have a much longer list of positive role models than I do of negative ones. However, my concern about role modelling is that those people with little integrity or with the *'What's in it for me?'* approach are often in a position where they can dominate staff who have either not yet encountered their own positive role models or not developed their own leadership skills. It is imperative that we keep nurturing those who *'Keep the important thing the important thing'* and model the way for others to choose the positive role model route. I dare not list my own positive role models for fear that I leave someone off the list, but as you know what is important, you will know who you are. Furthermore, I do not imagine those *'What's in it for me?'* types reading my book!

So now I reflect upon my impact on others; what is it about me that ensures good/positive role development and provides opportunities for others? In a later chapter, I am going to look at feedback I have gratefully accepted and recognise its impact on my behaviour; however, just here, I am thinking about myself as a leader.

When I was Senior Sister in my unit, I heard one of my Junior Sisters advising a new staff nurse.

"Louise is fair and will support you; she knows what she is doing, but do not cross her."

I remain unsure of what it was that staff thought I would do if they 'crossed me,' and I tried my very best not to be scary. I sought to lead with respect and not fear and to be honest. If I was 'crossed' or 'cross,' it was usually with surgical colleagues or the management team - not to generalise across groups of staff but just saying it like it is!

With my interest in education and development, it was always my approach to ensure that everyone had the opportunity to do something. It was impossible for everyone to do something at the same time, but it was totally possible to provide opportunities to everyone by being responsive to their interests and strengths. Whatever 'it' was, of course, must be relevant to the service for our patients, so flower arranging, whilst relaxing and creative, was never an option. Planning development for staff included formal, academic, whole qualifications such as degrees and masters, to diplomas, stand-alone modules, mentorship, reflection, clinical supervision, conferences, journal clubs, teaching boards, standards and protocols and then later research and publications; all alongside accreditation as a Practice Development Unit - the first in Wales.

This type of role modelling, planning, and actively listening to staff built a team that few wished to leave; many sought to join, sickness rates were low, complaints non-existent, audits positive, infection rates low, morale high and standards of care the highest possible. Of course, education and development are not the only things needed. An understanding of staff and a flexible working pattern was also important. It provided another opportunity to role model the willingness to cover clinical shifts and to ensure that staff were salaried to work or time off organised within a short period of time. Most of the surgery was elective, so rosters could be planned and adjusted when needed. However, when emergencies arose, the need for staff to rise to the challenge was imperative; leadership and team working provided the answer every time, with the need for bank or agency nurses a rare event indeed.

When I left clinical practice, my leadership qualities were to enhance my own development and my ability to facilitate in-house leadership programmes as well as the Royal College of Nursing Clinical Leadership Programme. So much was learnt about the impact on others, and to see nurses realise and recognise their own strengths and apply this to their practice was incredibly rewarding.

One group of nurses and midwives that I facilitated through a short leadership programme wrote a poem for me and had me read it when the Chairman came to present them with their certificates. It was both embarrassing and pleasing in equal measure; what a lovely way to receive feedback. The RCN CLP groups spoilt me with flowers and gifts as a way of saying 'thank you,' which was so generous and gratifying. I remember their learning and development and their recognition of my role modelling when I add their decoration presents to my Christmas tree each year.

I recognise that I have been fortunate to work with many very good people, and I am gratified that they have told me that I have positively impacted on their development, practice and many careers. I maintain that we all need role models; we will all follow others along the way. I am proud to look over my shoulder, figuratively speaking, and 'see' all those who have followed me - what an absolute honour.

Chapter Nine

Study and Work

"A positive attitude gives you power over your circumstances instead of your circumstances having power over you."

—Joyce Meyer

As student nurses in 1984, we were employed by the NHS from the start, we were rostered to work 37.5 hours per week, and we received a wage each month - £204 after paying for my room in the nurses' home as I remember it. Some students lived at home as they were close by, but the majority lived on the hospital grounds. When our placements took us to other hospitals, we packed up and moved there, moving back to base 8-10 weeks later. None of my fellow students had children or part-time jobs, and 80% of us were 'fresh-faced,' straight from school.

We worked hard, any shift, all shifts, split shifts, weekends and, during the second year, night shifts for ten weeks. We played hard, too, with busy and active social lives, but we also completed our studies and assignments at our dressing tables/desks in the nurses' home.

Since commissioned pre-registration nursing programmes switched from the small Schools of Nursing in the hospitals to the Schools in Universities, the format has been challenged, changed and updated on several occasions. The need for nursing to be a graduate programme has been debated, researched and written about plentifully and now, across the UK, nursing is a graduate programme. With many changes in provision and considerable flexibility, people can access nursing programmes through a variety of routes. This means that our now huge student cohorts are representative of all genders, socio-economic backgrounds, educational backgrounds, ethnicities, ages and from the UK, Europe and internationally.

For our students, this presents a rich and varied cohort with a vibrant and exciting workforce for the future and a challenging and exciting time for colleagues in the NHS, all other healthcare settings and in the Higher Education Institutes.

As we continue to support and mentor our students as per our university regulations, we also take on the role of Academic Assessor and liaise with Practice Supervisors and Practice Assessors as per the NMC Education and SSSA (2018). These provide us with frameworks, guidance, standards and policies, but nothing can prepare us for all of the things our students will look for guidance with.

All universities have student experience, health and wellbeing, financial and student union services. However, when a student tells a nurse something, we require considerable willpower to refer them to someone else and not to help problem solve because soaking up problems and solving them is what nurses do.

Some of my colleagues in education may say they just signpost the student and do not get involved, but I know the majority of us will guide, question, suggest and lead them to the help they need rather than simply point them in the right direction and let them go!

I totally appreciate that students join the programme experiencing a whole variety of situations - getting married, getting divorced, recent bereavement, holding down a job, financial difficulties, married with children, single parents, pregnant, recovering from or living with physical or mental health conditions, requiring reasonable adjustments, additional learning needs or specific cultural needs.

It is a minefield out there, and we depend upon our students being open and honest with us if we are to help them, support them, problem-solve with them or signpost them. Equally, our students deserve, respectfully, for us to be open and honest with them. When students tell me how hard it is to work on placement, plus study, work part-time, care for themselves and/or their family, I must remind them that this is what they have signed up for. The only possible change in the future will be not holding down a part-time job when they are a registered nurse. However, that is not the case for everyone as many nurses work bank or agency shifts as well as their NHS contracted hours. Responsibilities with family may, of course, change, but for many, this will increase with childcare or caring responsibilities. Studying will never cease; the intensity and volume may decrease, but being a registered nurse entails a lifelong commitment to studying, learning and development. As I usually say to students, "*Get used to it!*"

At the point of registration, I was a registered general nurse, and there were options to study further if you wished to move into midwifery, mental health, learning disability or child nursing. I set off on my trauma/critical care/ITU self-designed rotation programme, taking on new builds wherever I went. It only took eighteen months, though, before I was directed through the PDR processes to gain my Common Core Certificate so then I could complete my diploma and then my degree. So, the part-time studying commenced, attending classes in the School of Nursing in the afternoon after an early shift or in the evenings before a night shift. Times were flexible, and as the hospital paid the fees, we were expected to get there.

I completed my common core module as the foundation for my diploma in the evening classes with a nursing tutor who would later become the

Chief Nursing Officer of the country – now, *there* is a role model. Modules on clinical supervision and research methodology would count towards my diploma, and then it was on to studying for my BSc (Hons) in Nursing. At the time, it seemed surreal to be studying for a degree, but, of course, now this is the normal route for nurses.

I studied for my BSc part-time over three years whilst working full time in a busy intensive care unit. I was also bringing up my young daughter as a single parent since getting divorced. Family support was massive; we would not have survived without Nanas and Grandpas.

I can really relate to some of the issues my students talk to me about, and whilst I do not share my personal life with them, I am empathetic to their situations. I would put my daughter to bed and read to her, often having a quick nap alongside her before returning to my table and studying for a couple of hours. In this way, I made my way through my degree studies and graduated with a BSc (Hons) 2:1, with my four-year-old daughter applauding in the audience.

So, ongoing CPD is imperative: firstly, to maintain our registration with the NMC but more importantly to guarantee that we remain up to date, safe and credible practitioners who ensure best practice and ongoing improvement. Ongoing CPD is not all about formal education and qualifications; there are many opportunities to learn from other practitioners in clinical practice from reading research, journals and books, from attending webinars, seminars and conferences. I have learnt from working alongside students and new registrants. There is also much to be learnt when teaching others, and sometimes, just explaining things reminds us how much we know and how much we have to share. Learning from feedback given by students and patients is another avenue for our learning and development.

Whilst studying for my MA in Education, I took the opportunity to apply for a Florence Nightingale Foundation Travel Scholarship. This was an excellent experience that enabled me to undertake research for my dissertation and share this information via conference presentations and publications.

Working and studying is challenging, and at some points in our life, it is more challenging than at others. However, it has a positive impact on our practice wherever we work and so positively impacts patient care.

There is much written about stepping outside of our comfort zone. For an introvert like me, this is a challenge, yet I have repeatedly done so and have always been pleasantly surprised by the positive experience and favourable feedback.

Recognising that you have things to share that others will be able to appreciate and use is the thing that has spurred me on to write for publication, to speak at conferences and indeed to put pen to paper to write this book.

Possibly my biggest step up and out of my comfort zone was to decide after thirty-four years to leave nursing in the NHS. This was massive: partly it was due to a degree of disillusionment and a little frustration, but in the main, it was about wanting to continue to make a difference and needing to change my direction again to do so. Let's not underestimate the courage it takes to walk away from something familiar, something comfortable, something relatively easy, something you know you do well, something that people want you to carry on doing and step into a different nursing role where suddenly you are the new girl!

Things do not exactly seem difficult, but they are strange, new, different, and not all comfortable. However, you can draw on previous experience and apply it to this new zone you have entered. That is where I found myself and quickly recognised I had questions to ask to ensure I learnt and got things right. I had questions to ask to make sure I did the best thing for my students, but I also had answers, insight and knowledge to draw upon that supported others. It was a brave thing to do, stepping out of that comfort zone, but what a fabulous kickstart to the next stage of my career as a nurse.

Chapter Ten

How Many Hats?

"To be 'in-charge' is certainly not only to carry out the proper measures yourself but to see that everyone else does so too."

—Florence Nightingale

My experiences as a student and as a registrant never dampened my desire to be 'Sister.' Now, some would say that is because of my 'control freak' tendencies; my mum always said I was bossy! Whilst I do enjoy being in control, I believe it is down to my organisational skills. These are very important to me; I love a list, a plan, a way forward, a timetable, or a schedule.

In my early days as a Sister I took a while to realise that my team could organise and get it all done in my absence; a sign of sound leadership, management and teamwork is when it all happens when you are not there just as it does when you are.

To this day I smile as I remember answering the phone for the first time, saying, "Hello, cardiac ITU, Sister speaking, can I help you?" What a lovely feeling.

Now, the role came with many challenges, but they did not dampen my enthusiasm; I had achieved my career target. I loved it, despite the challenges, and it remains my all-time favourite job. I had already worked as a senior staff nurse in two departments and commenced an MSc in Healthcare Management; I was ready for this job. At the point of going for the interview, there were many who thought I wouldn't get it, many who believed there was someone else in the running; however, they underestimated me. I was passionate, and I went to that interview with steely determination camouflaging my nerves and anxiety.

I am not sure who was the most surprised when the phone call came through that afternoon offering me the post - my goodness, there were some celebrations that evening!! I believe my readiness came through; I had management experience, clinical skills, and I was credible in my role. I was organised around human resources, policies and procedures, budgets and finance, politically aware and understood people.

The thing that some found challenging was my determination to seek and understand the rationale behind management decisions as well as clinical decisions. I have always sought answers to 'Why?' and anyone who knows me, including my students, will tell you that I encourage everyone to seek and understand the 'why?' behind everything we do.

So, when I stop to consider my Sisters post, my unit, my staff, my responsibilities, my challenges, my passion, and my drive, I always do so in the context of my team. No one individual can do everything, but as a team, we can do everything and pretty much anything.

As Sister, I wore many hats and was many things to many people. As a successful unit with low complaints, low infection rates, low sickness, high retention, and excellent outcomes, we were seen as an area of excellence. We were often 'wheeled out' for visits by external agencies and the Welsh Government, so a special hat was required for these visits: a fine balance between political awareness and an honest representation of all we were doing.

I was a manager, leader, educator, peer, adversary, disciplinarian, and a role model, but under all these hats, I am also a friend, mother, daughter, sister, aunt and an introvert. All my roles influence my attitude, care, empathy, determination, passion for nursing and kindness.

People remember kindness, and this is something that we can always offer, whatever the situation. There is no limit to kindness; it isn't something to ration. A simple gesture of making a cup of tea will stay with people. Both relatives and colleagues have told me, years later, that they remembered me always making the time to check they were okay and also taking the time to make them a cup of tea. There are not too many situations in life that can't be improved a little with a cup of tea. Whilst taking the time to ensure everyone has a break or a drink, there exists the perfect opportunity to observe the environment and behaviours and recognise what else people may need help or support with. Many a vital clue can be picked up when providing respite and a cuppa.

One evening, a surgeon came out of theatre. He had been in there a while; however, the whole team had been there too and not had a break. He wandered along to the kitchen and came back with a cup of tea - just the one for him. A gentle and quiet word saw him disappear and return with a tray of drinks for everyone. The responsibility to look after all of us sits with all of us; kindness costs us nothing but means so very much.

I believe that being open and honest with colleagues, being fair and treating all equitably makes it irresistible for people to respond in a positive manner and instils the benefits of kindness in a team. It is simply not enough to have these words written down in an organisation's philosophy or values. These words must be embraced, believed in and demonstrated through our actions, all of us always, and when we fail to show them, we must be supported if we need to be and held to account if necessary. This is not about blame; this is about actively doing the right thing all of the time.

So, I mentioned earlier my introvert tendencies; many who know me may scoff at this as they imagine I am an extrovert like them. No, indeed, my comfort zone is introverted, my preference is introversion, but my career pathway requires me to step up and be different from my preferences when I need to be. I re-energise through peace, through quiet and through reflection. Other explorations to gain a better understanding of myself and how others see me has come about through clinical supervision with supervisors who would challenge me. Also, via the 360-degree leadership process so staff from all groups had the opportunity to provide me with feedback.

One particular clinical supervision session still resonates with me now, some 20 years later. My supervisor was helping me explore my management of staff and a particular situation around supporting staff.

His blunt yet thought-provoking question was, *"Tell me, Louise, when will you stop breastfeeding them all?"*

Once we had both stopped laughing at his audacity, I explored my tendency to be parental when I really needed to respond to the team on an adult-to-adult basis.

This learning was developed further when my 360-feedback facilitator explored my report with me. It was a humbling and gratifying process as I had sought feedback from across all disciplines and from several colleagues that I had had discussions and debates with my pursuit of an answer to my favourite 'why?' question. Despite all of this, my report was extremely positive and included enlightening favourable feedback about my leadership. One comment from my facilitator, though, sticks in my mind even now.

"Louise, don't just provide them with the walking boots and sticks; let them look at the map. They will follow you anywhere, up any mountain, but you have enabled them to go ahead."

That feedback helped me recognise the need to formally ensure succession planning and give the map willingly to others so that they can lead and keep moving forward.

I have applied this approach time and time again.

When I worked in an education role before leaving the NHS, I actively provided opportunities to the team so that they may develop and use their knowledge and skills. This came to fruition as team members gained recognition and promotion and continued to go from strength to strength in a variety of organisations.

Chapter Eleven

Have Scholarship, Will Travel

There are so many ways we can learn and develop our nursing skills, but there are also many opportunities to do this with funding from a range of places. Two friends of mine travelled to the north of America with a Florence Nightingale Foundation (FNF) scholarship, and they encouraged me to do something similar. Funded travel seemed to me to be for medical staff and senior management staff, but I was soon to discover that this was available for all.

Whilst completing my MA studies, I looked at studying the facilitation of Schwartz Centre Rounds for my dissertation. The plan was to observe Rounds in the UK but also in Boston, in the USA, where they originated over twenty-five years ago. The application to the FNF was fairly straightforward, yet attendance at the interview was anything but. They asked some tough questions and used 'encouraging' lines such as *'Answer in one sentence, not a paragraph,'* and *'Come on, Louise, use that big brain of yours.'*

I walked out of there and headed for the train home with no confidence at all of being awarded the travel scholarship. What a surprise, they awarded me more than I had asked for, so off to Boston I went.

What an amazing opportunity it was to live in another city, another country, another continent and learn so much. I rented a ground floor apartment in a red brick building on a typical Boston street and met with the daughter of Dr Kenneth Schwartz, the founder of the Schwartz Centre Rounds. She gave me access to their teaching website and their Consultants who facilitated Rounds in the Boston area. I travelled around the city visiting sites running Rounds, and I met so many people. Boston is a fabulous city, with so much history, some wonderful things and its own tragedies.

Of course, Boston is quite a centre of learning, and just visiting Harvard made me feel studious. I went to Massachusetts General Hospital, where Rounds first started - what a huge place. As well as teaching facilities, it had its own museum with tributes to Florence Nightingale and exhibitions of equipment from long-gone times. I had the opportunity to stand in the original operating theatre and watch a reconstruction of the first use of a general anaesthetic. It's a strange one, but if anyone tells me they are going to Boston, I can recommend some great bars, including Cheers, restaurants, shops, parks, museums, and the oldest library in the USA. However, a top recommendation would be MGH and its museum.

I learnt a lot about Schwartz Rounds whilst I was there and saw how facilitation could be achieved in many ways - from a room of over 200 people to about 30. What an absolute privilege to listen to the stories of those people and truly appreciate the extent to which providing care can push many to the very limit. The need to care for ourselves and for one another cannot, and must not, be underestimated. Kenneth Schwartz recognised this from his view of the world as a patient. Never would this

Nurse! | Thirty-Eight Years a Nurse — Have Scholarship, Will Travel

self-care and reflection have been needed more than after the bombing in his city during the Boston marathon.

I had access to some recordings of the Rounds that were running in the aftermath of this shocking event and spoke with some of the facilitators about how different it was when the Rounds were covering such a recent and traumatic event. It helped me understand that as facilitators, we are required flexibility to respond to whatever is there in front of us. So I recognised the value of being able to think on your feet, being responsive and reflexive.

My learning consisted of observing Rounds, participating, facilitating and providing feedback in steering group meetings. I also participated in the 360 feedback for those facilitators who took me around their city and surrounding towns. My reflections resulted in publications, interviews and presentations at conference. However, the main benefit was recognition of the facilitator role and being able to share this with others in my own organisation, as well as with those I mentor in other organisations in the UK.

Of course, the travel scholarship got me to the USA, and by taking some annual leave as well, I did quite a lot of sightseeing outside of Boston. I visited Cape Cod and went whale watching, which was very emotional, took a very small plane (both exhilarating and terrifying in equal measure) down to Martha's Vineyard, a bus ride to New York City for a couple of nights, visited Salem to get in touch with my witchy side, did a sailing trip off the coast where the Perfect Storm was filmed, went horse riding and bear watching in New Hampshire and rested by the coast in Maine.

Whilst there is work to do with any funded trip, I cannot recommend it highly enough for your personal and professional development and a life-changing opportunity.

75

Chapter Twelve

Resilience

"You either get bitter, or you get better. It's that simple. You either take what has been dealt to you and allow it to make you a better person, or you allow it to tear you down. The choice does not belong to fate; it belongs to you."

—Josh Shipp

I am not wholly convinced by the plethora of theories suggesting that we can be trained to be resilient or that we should need to be. It might be the case, or is it just that we find the strength and ability to cope with challenges and that when we don't, someone or something is there to support us? Is this enough? Is resilience a trendy word for coping? When I think of being resilient, I consider my strength and drive to cope with challenges in practice. This is further supported by my being focused, brave, courageous and honest. All of these are the pieces of the whole, and I have drawn on these qualities both personally and professionally.

As outlined in previous chapters, I have dealt with difficult working relationships with colleagues, as well as traumatic and emotional situations for patients and their families. These experiences have built my coping mechanisms and my approach. Our professional and personal lives are not totally separate entities; they are both a part of us, and one impacts the other at many points throughout our lives.

My first experience of being a patient came when I was a student nurse and on other occasions since. When you are a patient, there is very little chance of drawing on things and representing yourself; you realise how vulnerable you are as a patient and how important the nurse's role is as your advocate.

When you are a parent/friend/relative/visitor of a patient, however, it can be irresistible to seek information and adopt a nursing role as opposed to the relative/friend etc. This is even more so when you have concerns about the treatment or care that is being provided.

It is a difficult balance to strike when you are accessing services. When my own mother was once admitted for elective surgery and, on another occasion, for surgery for cancer treatment, I was made aware that ward staff had been 'warned I was coming.' This made me feel quite unwelcome on the ward and reluctant to question elements of mum's care; in turn, she wondered if she was going to be treated differently from other patients. Of course, when faced with things that my mum needed, I did undoubtedly challenge, and the care she received was very good. Nurses really should not feel the need to be defensive with one another; indeed, I was happy to help my mum with her personal care and provide fruit, cakes and chocolates for the staff on duty.

I have experienced a variety of challenges and tragedies in my personal life. These have impacted on my approach to life in general and my role as a nurse in particular. There may be times when we must be more forthright in our approach as nurses 'off duty.' These situations have led me to step in, for example, when a friend of mine was in a peri-arrest state, and I saw something that the medical and nursing team had missed. This was an incredibly unpleasant and emotional situation but led to a rapid improvement in my friends' condition and was the start of a number of changes to her plan of care.

I alluded earlier to being the friend/relative and not the nurse, and when my mother-in-law died suddenly, it took me until the day of the funeral to realise that we had not questioned what had happened. It was several months later, following on from conversations with medical staff, executive staff and then representatives from the whole department, that as a family, we realised that her death might have been prevented if things had been done differently and sooner. There is a very real need to learn from these situations and prevent them from happening again. When you are close to someone, it is not always possible to act in the way that perhaps hindsight tells you that you might have. Of course, when tragedy occurs, you are left shocked, and I felt a whole gambit of things, including shame, anger, horror, guilt, disbelief and great sadness.

The loss of my first daughter when I was seven months pregnant was heart-breaking but gave me insight to support others in similar situations, most especially when staff I managed experienced loss like this. I was truly able to empathise; however, I would not necessarily share my loss with them as this would not always be appropriate. As nurses, we can empathise in many situations drawing on our own experiences and feelings. This needs to be done with a level of emotional intelligence and the ability to recognise our emotional responses, to be self-aware and communicate appropriately.

As an adult nurse, I have, over the years, developed a greater understanding of mental health, and awareness of it is heightened in society more generally. This knowledge and understanding enables nurses to approach their patients with a complete, holistic approach, considering how other things impact on their physical wellbeing and indeed their compliance with treatment and planned care.

Just after my 50th birthday, I was to pull on all my strength, drive, knowledge, courage and, above all, love when faced with a traumatic situation that led to mental health issues for my daughter and, though much less seriously, for me too. She had been repeatedly assaulted by someone that I thought I knew: someone I believed I could trust and would never have considered capable of such a thing. These revelations rocked my world and changed everything forever. However, first and foremost, my role as a mother was to ensure the safety and care of my daughter. I had to support her through a plethora of situations, including police, legal advice, hospital admissions, accessing emergency and non-emergency mental health services - just to be there for her every step of the way.

Through all of this, our family and closest friends formed a cocoon around us, providing love, support, kindness and, when it was time, laughter. I slowly realised that we had the strength to get through this, but the things I learnt about legal matters, investigations, safeguarding, provision of services and vulnerable people were immense. What I thought I knew about depression, eating disorders, self-harm and anxiety was just the tip of the iceberg. It is more than knowing stuff, but actually thinking it through and knowing how we can support others, and ourselves, to survive these issues that will enable us to continue to move forward. So much of my learning and experiences came from observing and listening to my daughter, looking at some of the things she was reading, finding my own reading and looking at conversations on social media, particularly blogs. This learning gives me the strength to support others, to consider the things people have experienced, understand how they feel and perhaps why they feel like that.

As a naturally 'problem-solving and doing' nurse, I have now developed and honed my active listening skills that ensure that I listen with interest and fascination. I listen to hear and not necessarily respond by speaking to acknowledge, yet continuing to listen. My daughter has helped my learning, and many will benefit from my quiet attention and my absolute passion to understand, be kind and help where I can.

Chapter Thirteen

Being an Educator - as a Job!

"Great teachers engineer learning experiences that put students in the driving seat and then get out of the way."

—Ben Johnson

Through my clinical roles, I have always enjoyed teaching and loved to work with a student or a new registrant. The thirst for knowledge allows us to recognise how much we know, things we take for granted, things we do with intuition and muscle memory. Of course, when your student wants to understand the why behind the what or how this can be challenging. There is a difference between knowing what to do and how to do it, but without asking 'why?' we cannot understand the rationale for doing it. There is also a difference between knowing something and being able to articulate it so that others may learn and also gain that understanding.

I always encourage those I teach to ask 'why?' and sometimes this has come back to haunt me, for example, 'Why do we fold the sheets into those hospital corners?' Well, of course, bedmaking was drummed into me as a student nurse. Matron or Sister would often come on to the wards to check on the neatness of the bedmaking right down to the beds' wheels pointing in the same direction and the open end of the pillowcase facing away from the door. Naturally, these sorts of habits die hard, but much of it was related to keeping the beds clean, free from dust and the sheets straight to prevent creases and pressure damage. Could I think of that rationale when asked 'why?' Well, not immediately, but it came to me whilst the group of students came up with their own ideas.

Teaching in the clinical area is very rewarding and enables a growth in the confidence of the learner. They start to see that what at first seemed beyond them becomes something they can do. More than doing, they understand when things need to happen, why they are needed, what could go wrong and the impact we have on our patients. Educating others is a requirement of our NMC Code. Every nurse will have been or will be taught by other nurses as it is our responsibility to support the development of others and the ongoing development of our profession.

Whilst clinically-based staff may see students as a drain on their time, they are missing a trick. A well-supported, educated and confident student not only benefits the clinical area but is invaluable to patient care and contributes so much to the team that they are temporarily placed with. As a manager, I ensured that students left the unit with either a desire to come back and work with us or, if ITU was not for them, they would recommend the unit to their peers. This way, problems with recruitment dissolve and many areas could learn from that.

Of course, once you have recruited new registrants, the education and development must continue because staff who feel valued and supported will stay. It is imperative that staff feel safe psychologically, that they know the team will look out for them, and that each will watch out for the others. This safety impacts positively on the retention of staff and upon patient care. If you asked a member of such a team, *"Why did you do that for your colleague?"* the reply would be, *"Because I know they would do it for me."*

When I left the clinical role, my first formal role as an educator was that of a Practice Development Nurse (PDN). This role covered several specialities across the then Trust. Whilst it gave me time to develop and provide sessions around management skills and leadership, it also exposed me to organisation-wide issues and potential for development. Working with colleagues, we developed documentation, study days for IV medicines, safeguarding, infection control, risk management and many others. Being in a position that could influence Sisters and Junior Sisters and also look at succession planning was to become something that would lead to my involvement in a national piece of work. This was around Empowering Ward Sisters and then facilitating the RCN Clinical Leadership Programme in my organisation.

My next step was sideways or maybe even backwards when a change in management saw my organisation decimate the education and development provision for the nursing workforce. The majority of PDN roles disappeared overnight, with redeployment into a Senior Nurse being my next step. This was to be a difficult time as I believed I would lose all the work I had been involved in. However, the post itself did have some benefits as I was able to translate the theory of empowering Ward Sisters into practice in my areas of responsibility. I could bring to bear my management skills and deal with some performance issues that had been allowed to go on for too long and still made some good working relationships and a couple of lifelong friendships along the way.

My passion remained in education, and I saw and seized the opportunity to apply for two part-time posts - one with HCSW development and one in nurse education. Success in those interviews set me on a path of learning and development of my own that culminated in being the Lead Nurse for Education over some eight years. This role took in involvement across a now huge organisation and all fields of nursing and midwifery in one form or another. What an absolute privilege it was to be involved in the development of hundreds of staff from the HCSWs to lead nurses and to indirectly influence hundreds more by working with therapy colleagues, pharmacists, medics, ODAs, learning and development, local councils, the Welsh Government, RCN, NMC, FEIs and HEIs. It was not my favourite job, as that remains as my role as Sister; however, this was a close second owing to being able to influence and make a difference.

A massive challenge, due to lack of resources and input at an early enough stage, was the preparation of international nurses to take an exam that would see them gain their NMC registration. This was a huge undertaking from an organisation's perspective but also for me personally. I felt out of touch in the aspects of clinical practice that they were to be examined; plus, these were all experienced nurses either in their home countries or elsewhere in the world. I really should not have worried as the nurses were all extraordinary people. They had travelled such a long way, had already been tested on many aspects before setting off, and most importantly, they were all utterly delightful and a total pleasure to work with.

They were so respectful and hardworking, but they were also mischievous! Something about being brought together as strangers, living together and learning together, celebrating highs and accepting the lows. They had such fabulous love and care for one another but with added mischievousness, shown in the form of fun, jokes, socialising and sharing. Any initial anxieties I had dissolved, and the time I spent working with these nurses was one of the most rewarding times of my career. They brought out the very best in me and helped me realise that, at this point in my career, my mainly management and administrative role was not the best use of my time, energy, or passion, so it was time for me to move on.

Other things influenced my decision making as I was increasingly frustrated by the lack of value placed on education and development. The organisation had many priorities; however, a considerable amount of time was spent firefighting when issues arose. A better-developed nursing workforce with more effective leadership and a sense of their role being valued at a higher level could have stamped out those embers long before any manager would need to find the extinguisher.

So much research has been undertaken; indeed, whole organisations have been developed for the sole purpose of developing leaders and managers. Yet a look at the structure of the nursing workforce could show you immediately that the learning has either not been taken on board, not understood maybe, or perhaps completely disregarded. When you talk to nurses about leadership and management, everyone will agree about its value and the difference it makes. They can all provide you with an example of positive, strong leadership that they have experienced, and they can tell you how that makes you feel when compared to an experience of an approach that leaves them feeling disempowered, angry, undervalued, frustrated and generally negative.

Nevertheless, despite these conversations, it remains true that many senior nurses are negative about their staff, punitive when things go wrong, inflexible regarding change, and unreliable when asked for support. Many are unfair in their approach rather than equitable, resist sharing information that could help staff understand, cowardly when given the opportunity to disagree or debate decisions or plans, and most of all, the thing I mentioned previously, they are wondering, *"What's in it for me?"* I would suggest that this is the main thing that destroys psychological safety in a team and undermines positive relationships with staff.

Of course, some senior nurses do hold on to their values, passion and have developed positive leadership skills. However, the majority of these will leave the management roles and head off towards something more clinical, specialist, research or education. Or, if they do stay in post, they will stand out from the crowd, but these senior nurses are as rare as hens' teeth.

Chapter Fourteen

Being the New Girl

It is very strange being the new person, especially in an organisation where you know so many people from previous roles. Some I had worked alongside, some I had previously mentored or managed, some I had worked with when they were students, and yet here we were, all together in a team. Undoubtedly I had skills, knowledge and experiences that were transferable and would help me and others; however, I was not familiar with the policies, processes and systems.

Mostly I felt welcome, although there were a couple of people I was a little wary of. The one thing that was a little disconcerting was the expectation that I was a 'catch.' I didn't feel certain that I was as 'good' as people thought I was - I had a bit of imposter syndrome going on, to be honest. It probably took me a good few months before I started to believe in myself. I did recognise that my insight/experience of working in education in the NHS and previous partnerships with HEIs, FEIs, HEIW, RCN and NMC gave me something that others didn't have. This helped with my confidence and gave me the opportunity to demonstrate my worth and value to this team that I was new to. It wasn't long before more new team members arrived, and it was my absolute pleasure to be able to support them with things that I had been helped with.

Sharing an office with someone was something that I had not done for some time; however, my 'roomie' was superb and very patient with my many interruptions and constant questions. What an amazing person, a great nurse, mentor, teacher and friend.

There was much to be learnt by seeing others managing students' experiences and by observing teaching and provision of feedback. So much from corridor conversations or just popping your head around the open door of an unsuspecting colleague, saying, "Just a quick question," which could often take up an hour of someone's time. To be on the giving and receiving end of this type of situation enabled me to gain so much from others in the team and from the wider college team. This helped me settle in, learn and share, but oh how I wish I had made even more of those opportunities. The impact of COVID-19 was to change the very way we communicate with one another as well as our relationship with students.

I will always regret not making more of the time available with colleagues that we have lost. The tragic loss left an enormous gap never to be filled, and then some staff have chosen to retire during this time - I had not finished learning from them, and the sadness is significant.

There is certainly something to be said from making the most of every experience, every episode and living in the moment.

Working from home proved to continue for far longer than any of us would have anticipated at the outset of lockdown in March 2020. The impact on how we work and teach was to change things forever. As with any change, there will be benefits. Some of the adjustments in our approaches to teaching has led to embracing technology in a way that means we will probably never completely go back to our previous method. It also made us realise how we can make the very best of those teaching opportunities that need face to face and close work, especially for clinical skills teaching and assessment. This is not unique to undergraduate nursing programmes as there are so many other healthcare professionals involved in clinical care. It was quite something to see paramedic students practising resuscitation skills on the grass on campus rather than in the classroom, and why not? They are certainly not restricted to patient care indoors in their normal working day, but I am sure everyone was pleased it was dry and sunny that day.

Taking the majority of teaching online was initially a real challenge. Many people were discovering FaceTime, Zoom or Teams for their personal family catch-ups, and so this was becoming normal, which made it a little easier to engage. I found teaching larger groups of students online a less satisfying approach than engaging them in a lecture room when you could make eye contact or wander around to check everyone was okay. Teaching via an online platform is different altogether; however, for small groups of students or for small team meetings, it has quickly become normal. I am more than accomplished in sharing my screen and keeping an eye on the chat function - not bad for a virtual technophobe!

My facilitation skills have come to the fore. Supporting students with this new way of learning and helping them through their personal circumstances has drawn on many of my skills. Predominantly making the time to listen, being comfortable in making suggestions and ensuring we all have time to think and thus coming up with plans and/or solutions that suit individuals and/or the groups.

This approach has also proved essential when bringing colleagues together and enabling them to make connections that help us reflect. I facilitated a session for staff from across a variety of roles and groups to talk about their experiences during the pandemic and working from home. The feedback included, *"Your voice is so soothing, I could listen to you forever,"* *"You handled that so well, you set the scene, made it clear and a great summing up at the end,"* and *"Do you have any idea how good you are?"* This feedback helped me recognise my skills; I am good at what I do, I may be better than I realise, and I continue to make a difference.

Chapter Fifteen

Happiness

As we all know, life is full of ups and downs, and, as I discuss in Chapter Twelve, this happens both in our personal and professional life. Just as we must be responsive in our nursing role, support our patients and their families, guide and develop our students and new nurses, we must be responsive in our self-care too.

The revelation, nearly five years ago, of what my daughter had endured and kept from me for such a long time could have destroyed both her and me. Yet here we are, on the other side of that, and working on our happiness.

It would be more than remiss of me to suggest that such trauma can be dealt with and left because the impact is lifelong. However, how we allow that impact to influence us is our choice. The Josh Shipps quote at the beginning of Chapter Twelve tells us that choice does not belong to fate; it belongs to us.

Ruth and I made our choices, and we have come a very long way in the last five years. Ruth is now a graduate and is studying for her post-graduate Master's degree. She is a clever and beautiful young woman of whom my pride knows no bounds. She is working hard and looking forward to getting married to her loving, handsome and creative fiancé - Joe - who pre COVID-19 worked in the theatre and hopefully will soon get back to his creative art.

Joe knows Ruth's story (I hope one day she can share her story widely to help others), and he has signed up for the long haul! His proposal was super special; at the end of a showing of Pinocchio, after the audience had left, Joe called Ruth onto the stage. On one knee, he proposed and gave her the ring inside a smaller version of the wooden heart that he had made for Pinocchio. As Ruth accepted, it snowed on the stage! Thankfully one of the cast and crew filmed it all so Joe could share it with everyone; all of this on Christmas Eve. What a sore head I had on Christmas morning! They are a wonderful couple and are excitingly making plans for their wedding; I am not expecting anything too traditional.

Without the support of family and friends, I would not have survived the situation I found myself in, but now as a single, independent woman, I endeavour to look forwards. Joyce Meyer talks about the power of a positive attitude enabling one to be in charge of circumstances, as opposed to your circumstances having power over you. In my determination to be positive, I consider it important to remember: that was then, and this is here and now. I must, though, be respectful of my mental health and my wellbeing. I have had formal professional help and a lot of informal personal help over the last five years. With a tiny dose of pharmaceutical support, I have found the power of mindfulness and meditation to help me acknowledge the negative things, recognise them and then leave them. I am happy to say that I am mentally healthy and that the processes I have been through have taught me the importance of being mentally healthy is just as important, if not more so, as being physically healthy.

Everything that I have learnt throughout my life, especially in the last thirty-eight years, has shaped me as a nurse but, of course, outside of nursing and educating future nurses, I am also focused on happiness in life. The pandemic has certainly stopped many travel plans, but I have made a new friend who was the catalyst to me writing this book. We met just before the lockdown in March, and when he fell over and dislocated his shoulder, all my best A&E nursing skills came into play! Regular pulse check, arm elevated using a scarf in the absence of a sling and off to MIU we go. My on-scene diagnosis was correct, and the anterior dislocation was relocated by a very patient and skilled Nurse Practitioner. The use of Entonox gave us all many a laugh, and my calming encouragement led to me being told, *"You have the kind of voice you would want to hear when you are dying."*

Now, anyone who has seen the film 'Misery' will not miss the irony of an author being held captive for several weeks by a nurse, but, of course, he needed help. Besides, it was the Government lockdown that made him captive, not me tying him down or breaking his ankles!

Chapter Sixteen

2020 Onwards

"Taking care of yourself does not mean me first; it means me too."

—L.R. Knost

The impact of COVID-19 has been like nothing else that I have seen in my lifetime, and the same is true for the vast majority of us. My role in supporting my students has been difficult at times as their situations, both personal and professional, have required significant consideration and attention. Thank goodness the university has responded so well in its additional support of staff and students.

My eyes were truly opened when I participated in COVID testing students so they could be comfortable with their decisions to travel home for the Christmas holidays in 2020. The students and staff who stepped up to help with the organisation and then the testing of students was phenomenal and made a real difference to those who wished to travel home and to their families and friends eagerly waiting to see them after three anxiety-provoking months.

There were, and remain, some anxieties within my own family and friends about the pandemic and the isolation that many of us have experienced through so little contact with our loved ones. It has certainly highlighted how much we perhaps take for granted our regular contact and socialisation and how we must respond in different ways just now. Who knew you could have exercise classes, family quizzes, bake-offs, yoga, drinking parties, reunions and a good, old-fashioned gossip online?!

I responded to the call to arms from the NHS - not to return to work in a ward environment as it has been such a long time, and I really am not sure that I would be very much help. However, I have been back for some training and assessment, and I joined the immunisation workforce. What a fabulous way to make a contribution; I am so very pleased. I have played a small part in vaccinating, firstly, NHS and Social Care staff and then people from our community. Whilst contributing, I also made contact with many, many staff who I had worked with in the past and who had also returned from retirement to play their part. This has meant that I can continue to draw upon my nursing skills, and as John Magee said, *'I love the fact that nothing sets my soul on fire more than helping people.'*

Printed in Great Britain
by Amazon